THUNDERBOLT ODYSSEY

P—47 War In Europe

KEMAL SAIED

To Frank W. Kissel

Best wishes.

Kemal Saied

STONEWOOD PRESS
3107 Summit Blvd.
Sand Springs, Oklahoma 74063

THUNDERBOLT ODYSSEY

P-47 War In Europe

Second printing

Published by:
Stonewood Press
3107 Summit Blvd.
Sand Springs, Oklahoma 74063

ISBN 0-9624084-0-9

Library of Congress Catalog Card Number 89-51511

Printed in the United States of America

ACKNOWLEDGMENTS AND CREDITS ARE GRATEFULLY
EXPRESSED TO THE FOLLOWING FOR THEIR HELP.

My three sisters: Bedelia, Nell and Edna Mae, for their love and
foresight in saving my letters and returning them to me, giving me
the basis for this book.

Andrew F. Wilson, former squadron S-2, intelligence officer, and
404th Fighter Group public relations officer, for his kind
permission to use excerpts and photos from his 404th Fighter
Group's history book, LEAP OFF, an invaluable source of
information which confirmed dates of events that could be recalled
only by written records.

Kenneth W. Thomas and Charles "Lee" Smith, Jug pilots, for their
help in research and, more importantly, their encouragement and
support to continue my writing efforts.

Gladys Ivy, of London, who edited this book from the British
perspective, and tried to keep me out of trouble with our Allies.

Cover Photo:
Capt. R. M. Walsh's P-47 flying through the debris of a munitions
truck he had just strafed during the Invasion of France. This
dramatic picture was excerpted from the gun camera film of Lt. W.
Whitman's P-47 as he followed his leader on the strafing run.
(USAF)

Kemal Saied

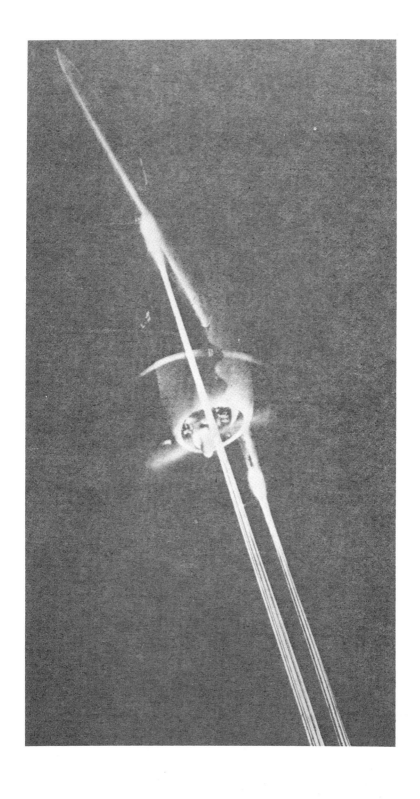

CONTENTS

THUNDERBOLT ODYSSEY

P-47 War In Europe

INTRODUCTION

Millions of men and women served in the U. S. Armed Forces during World War Two, each with unique experiences that could give insight into their lives during that period. Millions of others not in the service were also affected by the war, each of whom had a story to tell to give a better understanding of the overall effect the war had on a country and its people. This account of some of my experiences and thoughts during this period is viewed from only one person's perspective.

The period documented here is from the time leading to my departure for Europe until returning to the States after the war ended. This journal is based on my letters home and saved by my three sisters, without whose love, care and foresight this would never have been remembered in such detail, if at all.

Secret feelings such as love, God, death and the like were somehow easier to write about to a non-judgmental diary than to discuss verbally with anyone. Included here, in addition to the recreation of the letters, are personal thoughts not written in the original letters.

Reading the letters by date and location brought back a flood of details omitted in the letters because of censorship and other reasons. Memories long forgotten were recalled and included to make the story more complete.

These incidents are as accurate as possible, based on my memory, my letters home and research through personal and official Air Force documents.

Kemal Saied

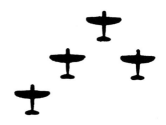

THUNDERBOLT ODYSSEY

P-47 WAR IN EUROPE

Kemal Saied

CHAPTER ONE

DECLARATION OF WAR

The mood of America in 1939 and 1940, when Germany's Adolf Hitler stretched his tentacles across Europe, was one of caution and anticipation. Caution meant wondering what involvement the United States would have in this global cancer. Anticipation was waiting for the other shoe to drop.

It was now 1941 and America was on needles and pins.

The Pledge of Allegiance to the flag was recited in every school in the country and flags magically sprouted on The Fourth of July and Flag Day, June 14th; the Star Spangled Banner was sung on special occasions and Americans didn't like Adolf Hitler. But an overt display of patriotism was not obvious. Yet, adults and children old enough to understand the threat of being under the domination of another country, had an underlying feeling that they would defend America's freedom, come what may, although the country was still in a desperate struggle with the problems of an agonizing depression.

The threat of war with Germany had accelerated during the past three years and now seemed imminent. The country was gearing up for a fighting war. Young men were being drafted into the military and assigned where they were needed most, but those enlisting voluntarily were allowed their choice of military branches.

My friend, Louie, had already received his draft orders to go, but he decided to enlist in order to choose the Air Corps. It was just a matter of time before I would be called, so I joined with Louie so we could give each other moral support during the war we knew was coming.

At this time the Air Corps was part of the U.S. Army, known as the U.S. Army Air Corps (USAAC). As part of the army, members of the Air Corps were called soldiers whether on the ground or in the air. Soon the USAAC became the U.S. Army Air Force, then later, the U.S. Air Force, a separate arm of the military.

Louie and I were sworn into the U.S. Army Air Corps as buck private soldiers, in the basement of the Oklahoma City courthouse in the morning of 3 August 1941, four months before war was declared. The next stop was Fort Sill, Lawton, Oklahoma, for three weeks of basic training before being sent to a more permanent place. I found out later after being assigned to almost fifty airfields, bases, camps and forts during the next four and a half years, that there was no such thing as a permanent post during a war.

Basic training consisted of rigorous physical training to put civilians in military shape and learn the rudiments of the service. Three weeks later Louie was sent to another part of the country and I was shipped to Ellington Field, between Houston and Galveston, Texas. We spent twenty–one days together then were sent to different places and lost track of each other until the war ended over four years later when we returned to Oklahoma to recount our experiences.

Nobody wanted a war, but the United States had been insulted, provoked and finally attacked by the Japanese at Pearl Harbor. The United States was then at war with Japan. Four days later President Roosevelt declared war on Germany. America was now at war on two fronts.

That latent patriotism immediately blossomed into full flower in a country so recently divided by severe depression and economic strife. Most able–bodied men not in work critical to the war effort, either rushed to join the armed services or waited their turn to be drafted. Others too young to be in the military sometimes lied about their age to sneak in. Others too old or not healthy enough for the military volunteered to do anything to help win this war. Some women were allowed in the military. Those left behind volunteered their services in any way they could, including taking jobs in factories traditionally held by men and proving their pioneer spirit again. The mood of the country was that the harder one worked, the quicker the job would get done and the soldier boys would come back home.

Patriotism was no longer just a word–it was a national emotion.

Being in the military had its good points as well as bad. Those of us lucky enough to return home saw a lot of the world we would not have seen otherwise, and did things we wouldn't have done back home. Some good, some bad, but it all contributed to a young man's maturity. Living under conditions never encountered as civilians taught us to live with and help one another, made truer friendships and even made some situations bearable.

Brothers Jimmie, Bill and Cecil had also entered the military early in 1942, but Ralph spent one day in the army before being disappointed to learn that he didn't pass the physical. Jimmie had been in the National Guard for several years and his division was called into active duty. Bill and Cecil were drafted into the newly named U.S. Army Air Force. Now the four brothers were scattered throughout the world and Ralph served by working at Tinker Field, the Air Corps maintenance depot in Oklahoma City. Sisters Bedelia, Nell and Edna Mae stayed at home with Mama and Papa to do what they could for the war effort from there.

Now that the family was separated we felt closer than when we lived together and sought that special family relationship we didn't realize existed until now. We wanted to keep track of each other and devised a system to do it. One of the many rules of censorship for servicemen was that their exact location could not be revealed in letters for fear the enemy could intercept the mail and deduce the location of military organizations and guess their approximate strength. So it became a game to try to locate each other by hints, key words and phrases in letters which only the recipient could decode.

Home would be the clearinghouse for information which was then dispatched to the others, and perhaps another piece of the puzzle would fall into place. Mail was so slow that just when a location was almost determined, a letter would arrive telling of a move to another location and the search would begin again. It was frustrating.

I had built balsa wood model airplanes as a kid and, as most thirteen–year–olds, I had a goal in life. Mine was to fly real airplanes. I didn't dream I would actually fly fighter airplanes in the Air Force.

Drawing airplanes in the margins of my eighth grade history book didn't help my grades any, but getting through the eighth grade and high school and two and a half years at the University of Oklahoma were enough prerequisites to apply for the aviation cadet program.

Tuesday 17 November 1942

I had applied for aviation cadets in February before joining the USAAC in August and failed the physical. A second application was withdrawn at my father's request (he was afraid I would kill myself flying). Now a staff sergeant in Alaska, my desire to fly flared again and my third application was submitted and accepted. After a preliminary physical examination in Alaska, my commanding officer wished me luck and sent me back to the States with his heavy parka as his parting gift. From then on, it was an uphill battle to keep from washing out.

The only reason I applied for aviation cadet training was to fly, and as long as I was in the military, I might as well do something I would enjoy.

Tuesday 10 December 1942

By the first of December, I was in preflight. The aviation cadet program was divided into four phases: preflight, primary, basic and advanced. Preflight consisted of a series of mental, psychological and physical evaluations to determine suitability for flying. Classroom instruction, or ground school, was included. Cadets surviving preflight were forwarded to primary flying schools for their first taste of flying. Others were dropped from the program and sent to schools more suited to their individual skills.

Wednesday 2 February 1943

Primary flying training at Tuscon, Arizona, was the first big step for aviation cadets, the real test of flying ability.

In preflight, the Link Trainer put me in the cockpit. I also had the pleasure of sitting in a real airplane at times, but not until now was I to be a part of the airplane. The civilian instructor didn't have to coax me to jump into the cockpit of the little plane. I was now going to be a real pilot.

Every day but Saturday afternoon and Sunday, daylight to dark, was filled with ground school and flying which were alternately changed from morning to afternoon. The early morning air in the Arizona desert was smooth but the hot afternoon sand, especially near the ground, tossed the light primary trainer around like a leaf in the wind. It was a challenge to land for a beginning pilot. I kept it a secret that I got airsick bouncing around in the traffic pattern coming in for landings. Repetition of landing finally worked the airsickness problem out.

Each step of the training periods, from preflight groundschool, then into primary, was a new dimension. The PT–22 was the first plane I had ever flown, a powerful machine to me because it got me into the air. There was nothing to compare it with, and I loved it. The adventure of flying was indescribable.

There being no radio in the PT-22, green and red lights from the tower's biscuit gun were the signals to either land or takeoff. Green for go and red to wait for further permission. The instructor's voice was transmitted from the front cockpit to the student in the back via a Gosport tube, a primitive arrangement of the instructor speaking into a rubber tube that carried the voice into the student's earphones. That was a disadvantage to the student because he couldn't talk back.

The instructor also used hand signals in addition to the Gosport tube. When the instructor wanted the student to take over the controls he simply held his hands in the air in view of the student, indicating he no longer was flying the plane. The student then had control. If he was not attentive at the moment, the instructor would wiggle his control stick, which also moved the student's stick, to get his attention. If that didn't do it, he would wiggle it enough to hit the student's knees.

Wearing the goggles and helmet of a pilot was the badge of an elite fraternity, but until we soloed, the goggles were worn around the neck while on the ground. The day would come when we would solo and be allowed to wear the goggles above the eyes while not in use, signifying to the world that we were "hot pilots."

The thrill of flying became a reality, and I was satisfied with everything about the little open-cockpit two-holer. Now it was time to go to basic training for the bigger plane.

The wash-out, or failure, rate was high in primary but those completing that phase went on to basic training at another field. I was sent to Pecos, Texas.

Tuesday 27 April 1943

From the Arizona desert to desolate West Texas was not much of a change in the weather but flying in a more powerful airplane was much different.

The enclosed greenhouse canopy of the BT-13 basic trainer gave the feeling of being in a "real" airplane. The big radial engine showed off its power to the novice pilot by spewing smoke and shaking violently when it was cranked up. It had more instrumentation and its own battery, unlike the PT-22 that had to have a mechanic crank its inertia starter. And the BT-13 had a radio so the student could speak to the instructor and communicate with the tower and other airplanes in the air.

This was a sophisticated machine to a primary cadet. Formation flying, cross country flights, instrument flying, night flying, navigation and acrobatics made basic more like flying.

The BT-13, basic trainer, made by Vultee and named the "Valiant" by the Air Force, was affectionately called the "Vultee Vibrator" by all who knew her. It earned its nickname as it was a noisy airplane with built-in features to make it a more difficult plane to fly than either the primary or the advanced trainer. The primary trainer was necessarily an easy plane in which to teach prospective pilots the basics. After fighting the controls of the Vibrator for three months, we would find that the AT-6 advanced trainer with its smooth handling, would be a pleasure to fly.

The Vibrator didn't want to turn as easily as the primary trainer, but the added trim tab controls helped. The torque from the high-horsepower engine, especially on takeoff, wanted to turn the airplane to the left, so the use of heavy right rudder was called for, and the muscles in the right legs of pilots often got more exercise than the left.

Three months of gruelling ground school and flying qualified those who passed to go on to advanced. My next stop would be Luke Field, Arizona, where most single-engine training in the West Coast Training Command was taught.

Wednesday 3 November 1943

By now everyone was familiar with all types of aircraft: fighters, medium and heavy bombers, cargo and even navy aircraft. So toward the end of basic, cadets had the choice of single-engine or twin-engine advanced. Most chose single-engine, but even that didn't assure them fighters later on. I chose single-engine, and from that time on I expected to go on to fighters.

The AT-6 was a slick-looking airplane with retractable landing gear. This was the same airplane some smaller countries used as fighters, and America was using as a training plane. Stories abounded about the AT-6: it had half again more horsepower than the BT-13 and was smaller; how it could do acrobatics better than the BT-13; how much easier it would be to ground loop because its landing gear was narrower. A .30 caliber machine gun was mounted in one wing for strafing practice, and bomb mounts were installed under the wings for practice bombs.

With each phase of training, we became more confident and more comfortable with the progressively more powerful airplanes. The PT-22 was now a grasshopper, not the powerful machine it once was. The BT–13 was not the same airplane it was three months ago. But the AT–6 was a slick speedster. What could be better than flying an AT–6 from now on?

Ground school was tough but my flying was at least average, and after twelve months of intensive training, the United States Army Air Force had another second lieutenant with silver wings. My goal had been achieved, but it only whetted my appetite for more flying. I thought the greatest pleasure in life was flying.

Two orders were issued the day of graduation from advanced: one, promotion from aviation cadet to second lieutenant; the other, assignment to instructor's school. Then upon completion, as instructor in BT–13s. Back to flying the Vibrator again. It seemed a step backward at the time but dues had to be paid. Maybe someday, fighters.

Tuesday 6 January 1944

The next stop was Central Instructor School in Texas, then an assignment as flying instructor in California. Minter Field, California was a basic training airfield where the second step in the three–phase aviation cadet flying program was taught. That was where W. H. "Sully" Sullins, Jr. and I met and became inseparable friends in the service. He entered the service from Henryetta, Oklahoma, where I had also lived as a child. Two guys from the same small town and, to bring our relationship even closer, our fathers had known each other years before, even if Sully and I had not. We had promised our parents we would take care of each other. Don't worry, we assured them, we'll always be together. And we were.

Instructing flying was an easy assignment, although physically tiring and stressful.

The schedule for instructors was from noon to noon, including night flying, off the next twenty–four hours then back on again. It was a good life, but somehow it wasn't what I had in mind when the aviation cadet application went in a couple of years back.

For diversion from the humdrum, on our days off, Sully and I would get a couple of planes when they were available and bore holes in the sky just for the fun of it. Shooting each other down dozens of times and touching wing tips in flight proved, to us at least, that we were hot pilots. The school commander probably would not have agreed with us but he did agree that more flying time made better pilots and so encouraged off–duty flying.

We had been instructing for three months and getting itchy to move on. Sully and I let it be known that we hoped this instructor's job would be temporary because our hearts were set on flying fighters and nothing short of that would satisfy us. Bob "Robin" Grout joined us to make a trio who wanted to get off this merry‐go‐round. Others who felt the same way came forward to express themselves, and our group of dissidents now numbered nine.

The maneuvers that a high‐horsepower single‐engine fighter plane could do were exhilarating to a young man full of vinegar. Flying straight and level was for the four‐engine throttle jockeys, not me; and getting into combat would give me that outlet. I wasn't so eager to get shot at, but I was given this expensive training to help win a war, and flying was the best way I knew how.

D‐Day, the Invasion of France, was still a month away and reported daily in the newspapers and radio, and assumed to be imminent. We didn't know how or when it would occur but we wanted to be a part of it.

Wednesday 31 March 1944

One day a request was posted for sixty‐four pilots to volunteer for fighter training. This could only mean replacements for pilots being returned to the States or lost in the war. The first one of our circle to hear of the request quickly spread the word among the others, so as Sully and I relaxed in the officers club, Robin came in with the good news. We all rushed to headquarters hoping the quota would not be filled before we had a chance to put our names in the pot. Luckily, we arrived in time and were all allowed to sign up together.

The same day we requested the transfer, orders were issued for us to go to Williams Air Force Base, Arizona. The next morning we were on our way to Williams to check out in P‐40s to get the feel of a fighter plane before being sent back to Minter and the instuctor's assignment.

The differences between the liquid‐cooled inline engine and the air‐cooled radial engine were stressed in the early stages of training. Each student can hear the same lecture and go away with different impressions of what he had heard. The cylinders of an inline engine are in line as the name implies, whereas the radial's cylinders are arranged in a circle. The one impression of the inline that stuck with me was that it would freeze up and quit if the coolant were lost through a puncture of the coolant line. Whether true or false, my choice was the radial.

All the trainers I had flown had radials and, without realizing it, I had gained confidence in them. I had never had an engine failure and didn't look forward to having one, especially in an airplane that glided like a rock. I don't know why this phobia was planted firmly in my mind but the thought of an inline failure bothered me a little. It is not my intention to criticize the inline engine, but to give my impressions at the time. One of my greatest regrets was that I didn't get to fly the P–51, one of the best fighters in World War Two.

The radial was bulky and difficult to see over while taxiing, but once in the air, visibility was good. When first started up, it coughed and sputtered. Then, seeming to want to quit, started firing with more coughing, one or two cylinders at a time, billowing smoke from the exhaust, until all were firing in concert. It then smoothed out to a distinctive masculine roar expressing confidence, ready to perform its duty faithfully. Stories were told of the P–47 with radials still working to keep the airplane airborne even after suffering serious damage. It was always encouraging to hear these stories.

Inline engines were a new breed to me, and when told that the P–40, with its inline, liquid–cooled engine, would be our transition from trainers to fighters, I was a little apprehensive. The P–39 and P–40 with inlines had been the fighter workhorses of the Air Corps early in the war, earning their deserved respect. Others had emerged to give a wider range of services, so the later fighters were the new toys most desired.

After having been accepted to fly fighters, the next transition from training planes was to be the P–40. The combination of an honest–to–God fighter airplane and the inline engine was both intimidating and challenging, but the adrenalin was flowing and the eagerness of youth prevailed.

The P–40 was a single–place plane and there would be no instructor to hold my hand on the first flight as in trainers, so there was a lot of getting acquainted to do before taking it off. There was ground school, of course, but the main emphasis was on flying. The blindfold cockpit check was required before even taxiing up and down the ramp to get the feel of the plane. Then the big day, the takeoff.

I was aware I was not in a trainer. This was a real combat–proven fighter I was climbing into, the same type aircraft that had shot down Japanese aircraft, and now, I would be flying one just like the big boys.

It was a comfortably snug sensation when the throttle was pushed forward and my back was pressed hard against the back of the seat, unlike any other takeoff before. The concern about the coolant system failing was forgotten and the awareness of power was exhilarating. The ten hours given in the P-40 was not enough to make the pilot and plane one unit, but enough to give a taste of a powerful fighter airplane.

Sunday 30 April 1944

Having returned to Minter two weeks earlier to continue instructing, we wondered if the P-40 training was just a teaser. But yesterday, without warning, we were ordered to pack to go to Baton Rouge, Louisiana for three weeks of fighter ground school.

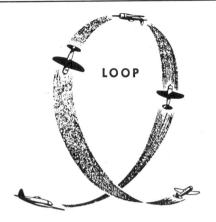

LOOP

CHAPTER TWO

FIGHTER TRAINING AND D–DAY

Wednesday 31 May 1944

Preliminary fighter ground school was completed and we arrived at Pocatello Air Force Base, Pocatello, Idaho, for P–47 flight training. The next few weeks were devoted to bonding the pilot and the P–47 into one unit.

My first meeting with the Thunderbolt came while still in advanced, with a demonstration flight across the runway by a civilian test pilot from Republic Aviation Corporation. He dove toward the end of the runway from 5,000 feet, crossing the threshold at close to 500 MPH. He flew no more than thirty feet off the runway for its full length before pulling up in a climbing turn for another run. Its thunder shook the concrete runway and the cadets' bodies vibrated in harmony with the 2,000 horsepower engine. After landing, cadets were allowed to look it over but not sit in the cockpit.

First impressions are lasting ones and most cadets who saw this demonstration made up their minds that the P–47 was their choice of planes to fly.

The P–47 Thunderbolt was referred to as the "Jug" because it looked like a glass milk bottle, but the British believed it to be a juggernaut when compared to their sleek Spitfire or our P–51 Mustang or glamorous P–38.

The Jug went through a series of design changes and modifications, dating from 1939, before being accepted by the Army Air Corps. Nearly 16,000 P–47s in fifty–four different models and sub–models were built during its production.

P—47D—10, 358th Fighter Group, an early "razorback" model. Later models were fitted with bubble canopies, giving 360 degree vision. Note the crew member riding on the wing, directing the pilot whose forward vision is obscured by the large engine. (U.S.A.F.)

Alexander Kartveli, its designer, incorporated many new features into the plane. The six—foot long engine helped keep any direct hit from the pilot, and was a safeguard in the event of a crash landing. A thick plate glass windshield in front, a steel plate behind the pilot and self—sealing fuel tanks below and in front of the cockpit were incorporated.

Most Air Force pursuit fighters in operation were small silhouette airplanes, but they lacked many features needed to compete with our enemys' fighters. Although the Thunderbolt was twice the size of most fighters and had almost twice the power, it also had more firepower than any other fighter. All that plus protective armor for its pilot, better altitude performance and protection for areas that were vulnerable in most other planes demanded a much larger package. It then became the largest single—engine, single—place fighter ever built. In addition to that pilot safety, a crash protector in the event of a turnover was installed aft of the pilot, and a crash skid was welded under the fuselage. That pilot protection plus the fire—power made one realize that it was designed with two things in mind: carry a lot of destruction and bring the pilot back safely. It was a pilot's airplane.

The side view of the P—47 revealed the same tear—drop shape as a free falling drop of water. It was not streamlined like the P—51, but nevertheless was an aerodynamically clean airplane and a handsome brute. Approaching the P—47 for the first time evoked the mental question, "how can this giant with the small wings compete with the smaller, more maneuverable, fast fighters?" I was assured, however, that it would perform as advertised.

Its reputation for reliability, firepower, range, altitude, obedience (it did anything the pilot asked it to do), loyalty (it seldom failed) and pilot protection (how we loved that protection!) had already been established.

It wasn't love at first sight but it was respect for its reputation and I believed all the tales about it. Sometimes love comes slowly but after one flight in the Jug, I knew this was the plane for me.

The walk around before entering the cockpit was the same preflight inspection taken with all other planes, but I noticed many innovations on my new partner. The purpose of the nose being over twelve feet in height was to keep the thirteen-foot propeller from digging into the runway while taking off. The wide-legged landing gear was a welcome sight after flying the AT-6 and P-40 with their narrow legs. The eight .50 caliber guns in the wings had the punch of a ten-ton truck hitting a brick wall at sixty miles per hour-so we were told. Whatever the comparison, it was more firepower than any other fighter.

Cockpit of a P-47. Before a pilot is allowed to fly the Thunderbolt he must be able to touch and identify every dial, gauge and control in the cockpit with a blindfold on.

Mounting the cockpit was aided by a toe step and a handle to get to the wing, then another toe step to climb into the cockpit. Once seated, the spacious interior was noted, and it was quickly realized that there was a place for everything and everything was in its place.

The controls, gauges and dials were within easy reach and handy to use instinctively, once familiar with them. The seat and rudders were adjustable for short or tall pilots, and everything seemed to fit any pilot.

Before being allowed to fly the Jug, the blindfold cockpit test had to be taken. It involved being able to touch every control and gauge while blindfolded. It wasn't just memorizing them from left to right. Any control or gauge the instructor called at random had to be touched. Eager to fly, it wasn't hard to do since we already knew the basics and where the instruments were supposed to be. But there were so many more on the Thunderbolt.

Next, the airplane was taxied up and down the ramp to acquaint the pilot with its handling on the ground. Now for the first ride. Solo, of course, as it carried a crew of only one. The instructor had done all he could and it was up to the pilot to do everything right the first time. Again, no instructor to get the pilot out of trouble.

When checking the magnetos at the end of the runway before taking off, the propeller gave an awesome tugging power as the brakes were held. The tail surfaces responded to the prop's whirlwind and the plane shivered with eagerness to takeoff.

Cleared for takeoff! The Jug was aligned with the runway and the throttle was smoothly pushed forward. The sound of the 2,000 horses had been heard before when others flew past, but it was overwhelming from the cockpit–especially for the first time. The three–point attitude and the big engine made it impossible to see directly in front. The airplane was guided straight ahead by travelling parallel with the edge of the runway as the roll began. The side view reference from the cockpit to the runway was kept until the airspeed allowed the tail to lift, lowering the nose enough to see over it. Visibility then became almost 360 degrees. The roar of the engine died down to a smooth hum as the landing gear were retracted and a climbing turn made.

The touch of the controls was much different than the other planes I had flown. The response to any movement of the stick was immediate except in a fast turn or dive pull–out. With practice, anticipating those maneuvers and adjusting for them became second nature. The seven–ton plane was heavy enough to resist much of the rough air and it did not easily toss around under thick cumulus clouds. Despite all the extra controls, it was an easier airplane to fly than any I had flown.

Just a few short minutes into the flight and after some basic maneuvers, the Thunderbolt's response to the controls was predictable. Instructions on this first flight were to feel it out, no acrobatics yet. Turn and banks, climbs, shallow dives and a stall or two (after all, this plane had to be landed). The luxury of power was appreciated. Constant pulsing of the engine permeated the pilot's body until engine and body seemed to have union with each other.

The job of controlling the prop from the cockpit was missing since the Curtiss electric prop was constantly adjusting itself for the proper bite for RPM and power settings. Only the airspeed gave the true picture and because the throb of the engine was constant, the pilot was only vaguely aware of the every–changing pitch of the propeller.

All the prescribed maneuvers had been performed and time was up, but it was hard to let go. A couple more lazy eights and a call to the tower gave clearance to land. The introductory flight in the Thunderbolt was over and the pilot and plane had bonded.

The plane was lined up with the runway on the final approach. With flaps and landing gear down, the Jug sank like a three–point rock but gave plenty of vision to see the targeted landing spot on the end of the runway. The first landing had to be perfect for all the men on the ground to see.

On the approach the decreasing speed raised the nose more and more until the center of the runway was lost under the big engine. The same guides for alignment with the runway as for takeoff were again used for landing. Keeping the edge of the runway in sight for alignment, the plane was held in a three–point attitude and floated, floated, floated in the summer heat, then THUMP! Perhaps it came in a little too high, but that can be corrected with experience. It was on the concrete in one piece. It was not a great landing, but adequate and would get better in time.

The crew chief congratulated me and was visibly relieved to see his precious plane come back undamaged. All smiles, I critiqued my flight: I'm a pretty good pilot.

Tuesday 6 June 1944 D–Day

"The infantry will have trouble enough landing and getting inland without being bothered by enemy aircraft. If your plane develops mechanical trouble,

> *come home. If a fight develops you will stay 'til the*
> *last enemy plane is driven away, even if you run out of*
> *gas and have to come down in the sea. If you run out*
> *of ammunition, ram 'em."*
>
> Col. Carroll McColpin, CO, 404th F G

Still in training at Pocatello AFB, we were unaware of what was going on in Britain at that time. We had never heard of the 404th Fighter Group to which we would eventually be assigned, but would learn of Colonel McColpin's high demands of his pilots in time.

The invasion of France had already been dubbed "D–Day," but the day and place were top secret to everyone except General Eisenhower and his immediate staff. Perhaps the President of the United States knew, but as far as Stateside America was concerned, D–Day could have been next week or next month, but it was now.

Sully, Robin and I were in the officers club when someone came in with the long–awaited announcement that the invasion had begun. We had hoped that we could be there for that important day, but General Eisenhower gave the order to go without us. The image we had in our minds that day was of a victorious war machine rolling over the enemy, when in reality, Americans and Britons were dying by the hundreds in the watery approaches and on the beaches in Normandy. We believed the end of the war was in sight and were more eager to go than ever before, but our training was not quite complete.

Wednesday 7 June 1944

Part of the ground school program at Pocatello AFB included having combat–experienced pilots talk to us in RTU (Replacement Training Unit) about what to expect in combat, and one of them, a major, told of his experiences in New Guinea.

The family was still trying to locate Jimmie, Bill and Cecil, and we kept our ears open for any clue that would help find them. Mail going overseas to military personnel was addressed to an APO (Army Post Office, or Fleet Post Office, if navy). An APO was a general area of a particular military unit and only a vague clue to its location.

Servicemen were prohibited from mentioning their exact location in outgoing mail or it would be censored before being forwarded. Quite a few letters were sent to the States with holes cut out of them.

Bill had been overseas a month or so and we knew he was in New Guinea but his exact location had not been pinpointed yet. After class I questioned the major about his APO and exact location in New Guinea. His APO and Bill's were the same and he confirmed that Bill's outfit was located near a village called Nadzab in the northeastern part of New Guinea. I was certain now that he had been located. After some letters back and forth to the clearinghouse at home and Bill, that was confirmed. Cecil was in Italy, Jimmie was somewhere in Europe and I was still in the States, so we could work on their locations.

Wednesday 26 July 1944

After flying in primary, basic and advanced trainers we were pleasantly surprised to find that the P-47 was easier and more fun to fly than any of our previous planes. This high-performance airplane had more controls and gadgets than any of the trainers. Attention to detail was more important to its operation and it responded to the slightest movement of the controls. It was a pleasure to be able to have charge of this 14,000 pound beast with precision.

The Jug had excellent handling characteristics and an unmatched toughness. This was the plane we were learning to love and respect. The Germans learned to respect it, too, in a different perspective. The destructive power of the Jug was well-known by the enemy. They even coined a special word for it. *Jadg* means to hunt or shoot and by combining *jadg* with bomber, coined the word "*jadgbomber*," then shortened it to "*jabo*." The warning cry, "*achtung jabos*" struck terror in them when they heard it as Thunderbolts approached.

Originally designed as a high altitude fighter, it was quickly found that the P-47 performed as well at lower altitude. It could carry heavy loads of armament as well, bringing its weight to well over seven tons. In addition, it had many other important features its pilots appreciated very much, like taking an enormous amount of punishment and still bring its pilot home.

A rugged ship, the Jug many times made it home with engine cylinders blown completely away or part of a wing or tail assembly gone. The ruggedness of the plane saved many pilots' lives.

From the latter part of April, additional ground school, including armament, air-to-air and air-to-ground gunnery, navigation, aircraft identification, maintenance and engineering, instrument flying, meteorology, communication and many other courses, had taken us from Arizona and Louisiana to Idaho. That part of our training completed, we were scheduled to return to Harding Field, Louisiana, and from there to the Port of Embarkation in New Jersey and on to Europe.

Whether we were proficient enough to go into combat would be proved later. We were familiar with, and had the opportunity to learn enough about the Jug to become a part of the machine, knowing that it would do its job. We believed we were ready for combat.

BARREL ROLL

CHAPTER THREE

OVERSEAS ASSIGNMENT

Wednesday 9 August 1944

Our clique of nine arrived at the Port of Embarkation in New Jersey a couple of days earlier. After a night roaming around New York City, we were herded up the gangplank of the former luxury liner, "Colombie." We expected to begin our journey within a reasonable time, an hour or so, two at the most. We were not familiar with the logistics of loading hundreds of men and tons of supplies aboard a ship for a two week cruise. First, it was to be loaded then wait for other ships to make up a convoy to cross the Atlantic together for safety against enemy submarines.

After boarding we were assigned sleeping quarters in alphabetical order. Grout's name was called early and he and another pilot whose name began with "G" shared a private cabin on B deck. When the assignments got down to the "S's," Sully and I were sent below deck to bunks stacked four high, no more than shelves on which to store our bodies for what was meant to be a night's rest. We counted our "roommates" by the hundreds.

Still in the harbor but, by military standards, no longer on American soil, we were therefore entitled to overseas pay. So we spent our first night "overseas" in the New York harbor.

All day and into the night under floodlights, the ship was being loaded. Morning arrived and tugs pulled the Colombie toward the sea past the Statue of Liberty. The decks were crowded with soldiers looking at the Statue, and those who could not get on the deck, took turns peering through portholes below. This was the first time I had seen her and wondered if it might be the last. No doubt, others were thinking the same.

Seven of the nine men who volunteered together aboard the Colombie going to Europe.

Monday 21 August 1944

From the time we boarded the ship and waved goodbye to the Statue of Liberty on the morning of 9 August, to the evening of Monday 21 August, when we docked in Liverpool, we spent thirteen monotonous and boring days playing cards and staring at the ocean.

This was the first time I, or any of the men I knew, had been to Britain, and we were awed by the new sights. There was no sightseeing during our first night in England as transportation was waiting to take us to Shrewsbury. We were to train there for another month before being assigned to combat organizations.

The quarters at the new base near Shrewsbury were half–cylinder Quonset huts, about a mile or so from the runways. The mess hall was about the same distance from us, but in a different direction.

In all our previous stations, everything: mess hall, officers club, barracks or ground school, was within walking distance, regardless of how far away they were. It simply meant that transportation would not be provided. The commanding officer at this base, however, issued bicycles for pilots to use, presumably to expedite our training. Whatever the reason, we liked the idea.

Friday 1 September 1944

> *"The Battle of France was won. In a scant week, the swift rush of the First Army and the British Second to the Northwest carried all the way to Brussels. Near Mons in Belgium the Allies sped by large numbers of German troops in a spectacular neck and neck race. The movement was so swift and so great that the 404th no longer could perform its tactical support function from Normandy."*
>
> *(Leap Off, 404th FG History)*

We had still never heard of the 404th Fighter Group, and their actions meant nothing to us yet. Almost a month had passed since arriving at Shrewsbury and the newness had worn off, but each day was different. We flew as much as the weather would permit, and sometimes when it wouldn't. And there was ground school again. In ground school and in actual flying, bad weather flying was stressed. Later, this extra training would pay off, but here at Shrewsbury, we lost some pilots due to the weather, who got lost over water. There were others who were temporarily lost and exhausted their fuel before they could get back to the base safely.

The subjects taught in the States were reviewed in detail again, in case we missed a point or two. Enemy aircraft were to be identified and the difference between enemy and friendly aircraft was to be determined in 1/50th of a second. Foolish mistakes were not tolerated.

Flak and flak evasion were explained in detail, as well as a healthy respect for it. Veteran combat pilots knew that flying through the black smoke caused by flak was safe because the fragments had already been dispersed, and only the harmless black puff lingered awhile. The only way to really understand this was to experience it, and the first time it was experienced, it would never be forgotten.

Replacement pilots listened intently to the old hands for fear of missing one small bit of information that might be needed later. We were now beginning to realize the importance of this extra training.

Pilots who had completed their tour of duty and were being returned to the States were given temporary assignments in schools to give first hand experiences to replacement pilots. It was comforting to know that at least some of the pilots did get to return home in one piece. Their actual experiences gave more credence to the information in the textbooks.

Death seemed almost incidental when combat – experienced pilots would talk and shake their heads in telling of incidents resulting in the death of one of their members. In the next sentence they would tell about the way an ammunition dump exploded when their bombs made a direct hit, and they flew through the fragments. The death of their friend was forgotten for the moment but would be remembered many times later.

A half dozen of us were heading toward the auditorium where ground school was being held when the identifiable roar of twin – engine planes was heard in the distance. Three A – 20s were approaching very low and we ground – bound pilots stopped to watch in envy as they passed overhead, playing follow – the – leader. They were so low that we ducked instinctively as they passed.

About 100 yards past us, the number three plane apparently saw a light pole directly in his path, and he pulled his plane into an abrupt climb to avoid hitting it. In the split second between the time he pulled back on the yoke and the time it took for the plane to respond, the plane mushed into the pole and its left elevator struck the top of the pole, tearing the elevator completely off. The right elevator was still in the climb position guiding the plane in a very short – radius half – loop, ending with the A – 20 heading straight into the ground.

We were stunned but did not run to the crash site. Knowing that the damage was already done and the pilot could not have lived through this kind of crash, it would have served no purpose for us to go and look at a horrible sight. One moment a man was enjoying his flight, and three seconds later his life was snuffed out. We continued on our way to the auditorium for another class on safety.

The next day we examined the site where the plane piled in and found it buried deep in the ground, the wreckage covering no more than a 150 – foot circle. It was learned that the pilots who buzzed us were celebrating their tour of duty in Europe and were letting off some steam before returning home.

Thursday 21 September 1944

Having completed thirty days of supplemental training, about 400 replacement pilots from various training fields in England were sent to an airdrome near Bristol. We assembled in an auditorium to be assigned to organizations now located on the Continent. About twenty organizations were to have their replacement pilots assigned here and forwarded to their respective units, wherever they were.

On the stage several field rank officers and some enlisted men were milling around a large fish bowl containing the names of all the pilots on separate slips of paper. The names were to be assigned by lottery to their respective units. It worked this way: a pilot's name would be drawn from the bowl by one of the officers and the name handed to the corporal who then assigned that man to his outfit. This would continue until all the pilots had been assigned.

Sully, Grout, Conway, Packer, Snyder, Sicard, Yocum, Webner and I had been funnelled this far together from Minter Field through several training stations to where we were now assembled. We had become good friends and wanted to stay together.

When the first of our buddies' names was called and assigned to the 404th Fighter Group, the rest of us gathered around the corporal who was assigning the names, and asked him to hold at least nine slots open for us in the 404th. Each time one of our names was called we would let him know to put us in the same group.

After about two hours of name calling and assignment, I was the only one of our clique of nine whose name had not been called. The corporal told us he had to fill out the 404th and couldn't hold the last opening for me. My future was at stake. If I couldn't be with my buddies I didn't want to go to war. The corporal insisted that he couldn't hold it and we insisted he could. Rank has its privileges and, with the offer of some American bourbon as a bonus, one space was saved for me.

The drawing went on and on until all the spaces in the 404th had been filled but one, and all the names in the fish bowl had been called but two, and mine still had not been drawn. I wondered if my name had been left out by accident or if I was being saved for some special mission. Perhaps my file had been lost and I would spend the rest of my life in Britain.

The next to the last name called was mine, and the corporal completed his assignments to the 404th, and the newly-assigned members of the 404th congratulated each other. We were still together, but this was just another step in the struggle to stay together until we would arrive at the 404th "Somewhere in Europe."

The unit's location couldn't be pin-pointed because by now the Allies were leap-frogging across France and Belgium so fast that the maps had to be corrected every few hours. Air ground support units were moving forward every time an airstrip was overtaken, staying in some places only a few days. At least we were assigned together. The next step was to get to the 404th and stay together.

Friday 22 September 1944

Yesterday we, with pilots going to other groups, were put on a train and sent toward Southampton where we were to board a ship for France. The Air Force never explained the way things were done, so there was no explanation why we were dropped at an anonymous rail station at the end of nowhere in Southern England.

We were directed to a valley where some pyramidal tents were set up waiting for us. Pyramidal tents which were to accommodate six men were furnished with twelve cots. Twelve cots in a six-cot tent didn't allow any walking space, and only the two men at the entrance could put their feet on the ground. The other men walked on other cots to get to their own.

After getting "comfortable" we were fed in the open field and told to make the best of the situation. Next morning we would be sent on to our port of departure, and then on to France. From there, to our assigned units, wherever they might be.

We were pleasantly surprised to find a shower stall set up in the field. The phrase "American ingenuity" meant a hot shower made from two 55-gallon oil drums hoisted on stilts, one holding hot water, the other, cold water. The plumbing beneath the drums allowed both hot and cold water to mix through a single shower head. This was a luxury not expected in this nameless place, and we took full advantage of it.

Still basking in the pleasure of a hot shower, we had to face the reality of the cold English weather which would make this one of the coldest nights of my life. The mysterious mix of cold air and that special humidity indigenous to only the British Isles combined to create bone-chilling cold weather. I had been stationed in Alaska in the winter and bore up under the weather quite well. It is different in England. Hardly ever below freezing, that special British air began by cooling the skin, then the flesh and then deep into the bones until they became brittle with cold.

The twelve tentmates decided to do something about the cold, so we fanned out into the field to scrounge some wood. The fog had formed three feet deep in the valley and was seeping under the closed tent flaps. Men seemed to be walking on their knees in the fog as we stumbled over mounds of dirt and vegetation hidden beneath the fog in our search for firewood.

Darkness came quickly and by the time we got out in the field it was quite dark. With the deep fog and the darkness we could only guess where to walk, so we felt our way through the field with our feet. When anything got in our way we stooped over and examined it with our hands. One of the men stumbled across a fallen picket fence submerged in the fog. That would be our warmth for the night. Another came up with a galvanized water pail in which to burn the fence.

Water pails were not meant to be used as room heaters as they didn't have draft holes in them, but beggars can't be choosers, and we did the best we could under the circumstances. So, by moving all the cots as much as possible, a small space in the center of the tent was cleared in which to place the pail. The picket fence was broken up and fed into the pail, but without a draft, the fire died out quickly. The only way to keep the fire going was to feed small pieces of fence into the fire a little at a time.

There were at least two things wrong with this system: (1) the fire was too small to do much good and only the hands of those huddled around the makeshift heater could be warmed, and (2) someone had to keep the fire fed continuously, so cooperation among the troops was necessary.

While four or five men warmed their hands over the bucket, they huddled together for body warmth. Each huddler, putting one of his two blankets over his shoulder while huddling, loaned his other blanket to a sleeper for his warmth. Sleep was non-existent, however, and the huddlers and sleepers were rotated often.

Finally there was no more fence to burn, so someone got the bright idea to use the center tent pole which was conveniently located next to the bucket. With the remaining embers of the fence still in the bucket, we somehow put the base of the tent pole in the bucket to be used as fuel. It made sense at the time. There would be continuous feeding of the pole into the fire. It relieved the operator of his responsibilities, other than to make sure the tent didn't burn with twelve men in it. By morning, the tent pole had burned down so that the tent had become one big blanket over all the cots.

What seemed a thousand hours later, morning came, and we boarded trucks for another tent city closer to Southampton where we were to board a ship to cross the English Channel to the northern coast of France.

Saturday 23 September 1944

We had left the States with several bottles of bourbon among us, rationing it out on occasion. But we had the foresight to save one full bottle to be used in celebration just before entering combat. The last night in England was chosen for the occasion.

It was almost as cold in that tent city as the previous one, so it was decided to make the best of the situation by going to a pub someone had told us about. That was the time to break open our last jug of bourbon.

The pub was about three miles by road and only a mile or so if we walked down the hill and across the creek, up another hill and then down the road. Either way, we had to walk, so the short cut was taken. Nine of us took off down the hill, over the hog wire fences, then to the creek, which was about ten feet wide and three feet deep at the crossing. The only way to cross the creek was over a ten-inch pipe traversing it. For the young and agile sober men crossing this pipe, it was easy. As we crossed, it was discussed what to do on the return trip when it would be dark, and our agility might not be as acute as at the first crossing.

On up the hill we went, down the road and finally to the pub. The natives treated us royally and with great ceremony as we opened the last bottle and shared it with those around us. The contents of the bottle and other drinks purchased contributed to the fellowship, and an enjoyable evening was spent drinking and singing.

Hardly anyone could carry a tune under those circumstances, especially Grout. His musical ability was so bad that he was asked to shut up, but he kept doing what he considered singing. Nevertheless, there was an evening of great harmony, we thought, and goodwill.

With the bottle empty and time to go drawing nigh, we said our goodbyes and left. The short cut across the creek was the route taken and the first one across the pipe made it safely.

Frank was the second to try the crossing. He made it halfway before a miscalculated step caused him to fall in the cold creek. Two others followed Frank and both fell at the halfway point. After that, the next in line said to hell with it and all the rest of us waded through three feet of icy water.

When we returned to the tents we were all cold sober and glad to have our cots and two wool blankets to curl up in. This would be our last night in England. The schedule for the next day was to awaken early, pack and be ready to board ship for the short trip across the English Channel.

SLOW ROLL

CHAPTER FOUR

ON TO EUROPE

Sunday 24 September 1944

The trip across the Channel landed us near Utah Beach, one of the sites of The Invasion of France. When we landed, wreckage of Allied military equipment was still half–submerged on the shore. It was a grim reminder of the slaughter that had taken place four months earlier, and we almost expected bodies to wash up as we went ashore.

It was cold and wet and early when we landed. Someone, somewhere probably knew where we were and where we were supposed to go, but none of us did. In the three years I had been in the service it seemed that there must have been a regulation never to give any information to the troops until the orders were given, and then, keep it a secret as long as possible. We were milling around, not knowing what to do.

Our leaders expected transportation to be waiting for us when we landed, but none was in sight. After waiting awhile to be told where to go and what to do, someone suggested that we strike up this road. We gathered up our gear and, like sheep, followed our lost leaders, slipping and sliding in the mud under the shifting weight of our baggage.

Eleven miles of walking convinced us that we had taken the wrong road. The trucks, overlooked back at the beach, finally caught up with us. A weary bunch of men, more used to flying than walking, climbed aboard for their next destination.

The truck gave us a tour of the beautiful Normandy countryside en route to our new temporary home in a tent city at airstrip A–9, near Carentan, about 40 winding kilometers away.

St. Lo was almost leveled and I could not see one building left intact. There were no bicycles nor hand drawn carts and the only traffic was military vehicles. This village had been home for some people and obviously a beautiful village at one time. Now the streets seemed almost deserted. There were a few women and old men sifting through the debris in search of something of value that might have been overlooked earlier.

I could not imagine what my life would be in that situation, but those people had no choice. I thanked God that I was in France protecting Oklahoma instead of in Oklahoma protecting France.

Bombed building in St. Lo, France.

We eventually arrived at A-9 to await our next orders to go to Paris, then others sending us to the 404th, wherever it might be at that time. We were to make the best of our situation here until moving on.

Tents were assigned and the rest of the day was spent locating the necessities of life, the water barrel, the mess tent and getting the bunks ready to sleep in that night.

Monday 25 September 1944

The day was spent in housekeeping and getting used to our new home. Six tentmates scrounged a wood burning heater and I found a straw-filled mattress left behind by another replacement pilot. We did not know how long we would be here and wanted to make our stay as comfortable as possible under the circumstances.

Shaving with cold water using a steel helmet as a wash basin. Morning scene in a tent city.

The schedule of the day was: rolling out of the sack at 8 o'clock, groaning and going back to sleep. Then, arising at eleven, I filled my canteen with water from a Lister bag, got my steel helmet, soap and towel, went to the back of the tent, and hunkered over a helmet wash basin and bathed as best I could with the equipment at hand.

The mess tent was next. The mess kits did not have compartments for different foods, so meat, beans, fruit salad and dehydrated potatoes, all from cans (perhaps the same can), blended into a one-course meal. By this time we were used to eating standing up or sitting on the nearest dry spot. It certainly beat eating beans and canned cheese directly from the can as we had been doing for the past week.

After settling down in the tents, eight of us went into Carentan to scout around. This was the first time we were in a country in which a language other than English was spoken, so it gave me a chance to try out my college French. It was easier to communicate than we expected, since sign language is universal and the little French I knew provided us with adequate communication. Some of my misused and mispronounced words caused a few laughs and broke the ice with the French people but they got the meaning.

When I asked a Frenchman how to say "it doesn't matter" in French, he gave the French phrase for "I don't give a damn." It took several conversations and a lot of shocked looks from the French before it was explained what it really meant.

Each stopover had been different than any other, and it was an education experiencing something new. Now, we had been assigned to our group and were anxious to get there. Next stop was Paris to get our final orders before going on to the 404th, so we tried to find a way to hurry the process. We didn't know where in Paris to go but that didn't matter at this time.

C–47s landed at Airstrip A–9 occasionally to deliver supplies and pick up shipments going elsewhere. Some of us greeted each plane as it landed, hoping to hitch a ride to Paris, but they all seemed to be scheduled for anyplace but Paris.

Early in the morning a C–47 Gooney Bird circled the field and came in slowly for a landing. When it landed we were there ready to ask the pilot if he was going to Paris. We were elated when he said yes but were disappointed when he said he was to pick up and deliver a load of K–9 Corps dogs and didn't have room for pilots. We considered ourselves hot pilots, sent over here to win a war, but when told that dogs had priority over fighter pilots, we wondered just how the war really was going.

Tuesday 26 September 1944
It was raining so we stayed in the sack and talked about whether or not we were glad to be stuck here for awhile while a war was going on just east of here. It was a carefree existence. No roll calls, no duties or responsibilities and no worries. We didn't have the comforts of home, but life wasn't too bad.

The only running water was when it ran out of a 55–gallon drum or a Lister bag into our steel helmets to be used for a cold shave. Still, life was pretty good. That rest stop was appreciated but our next concern was to get to Paris and our devious minds were alert for any way to get there.

Later in the morning someone came into our tent while we were still in the sack and said that a couple of men from the tent city had "requisitioned" a jeep from a vehicle depot near here. Robin, Sully and I decided that we should get a jeep and drive to Paris where we would get orders to go to the 404th. It never occurred to us that we didn't know whom to contact in Paris for the orders. But, what the hell, it was something to do, and it didn't take us long to dress and try the same trick.

We walked the short distance over to the vehicle depot and returned the guard's salute at the gate as we walked in. Once inside the fenced-in grounds, and hidden from the guard's view, we saw acres and acres of jeeps, half tracks, tanks and trucks of all sizes parked bumper-to-bumper. They were laid out in blocks of about 200 feet square, which allowed only the front or rear vehicles to be moved. We searched around for a likely piece of transportation. A jeep near intersecting roads was selected and I jumped in the driver's seat and it cranked right up. Robin and Sully got in and we backed it out of its space. Driving between the other vehicles, we laughed and hollered like a bunch of kids on a new sled and were having a hell of a good time. Everything in a war zone was expendable, including pilots, and who would miss one jeep out of the hundreds here?

I was not too familiar with the four-wheel-drive and Robin said he knew how, so I stopped the jeep and Robin took charge. Shifting gears experimentally, he managed to get it out of four-wheel-drive and aimed it out the same gate we had entered a few minutes earlier. When we arrived at the gate, we had become officers and gentlemen again, and the guard saluted us as we passed him. As we returned his salute he suddenly realized that we were the same men who only a few minutes earlier had walked in.

"Sir! Sir!" he yelled, "You can't take that jeep!" Robin speeded up and the guard's words faded out. Soon we were touring the beautiful French countryside. After sightseeing awhile, the next planned step was to pick up our gear and head for Paris.

When we got back to camp we were told that because of us and some others who did the same thing, there were road blocks on all roads out of the area. Vehicle's serial numbers were checked. The heat was on, and they intended to stop this crime wave, so we decided to postpone the Paris trip until the heat died down. The jeep was parked down the road near a hedge row and we retired to our tent to plan the details of our trip to Paris tomorrow.

Next morning the jeep was gone as well as our dream to drive to Paris by private vehicle. Perhaps the MPs recovered it, or some other soldier had the same idea. After having been thwarted, we still felt a sense of relief that we had not been caught. We didn't swear to go straight from then on but we certainly would be more careful of any future venture that wasn't by the numbers and in military order.

Wednesday 27 September 1944

Still at A−9 and planning our trip to Paris about mid−morning, we were killing time playing blackjack when orders were sent to pack and be ready when the trucks came to take us to the airstrip. We were on our way to Paris. If we had known we were leaving so soon we might not have taken the jeep the day before.

Each man had duffel, musette and B−4 bags and was living out of them, so when we were told to pack, everything was simply dumped into the bags and we were ready to go.

The planes had not arrived when we got to the field so we went to the mess tent to eat. By the time we filled the mess kits the planes had arrived and we rushed to board them, carrying our full mess kits. It wasn't easy eating out of a mess kit while carrying this much baggage and running to board a plane at the same time, but we tried. We finished our canned chicken while sitting on bucket seats in a C−47 Gooney Bird on our way to Paris.

Paris, hazy in the distance, came into focus as we came nearer. The Eiffel Tower dominated the skyline and the Arc de Triomphe and the Cathedral de Notre Dame were easily identified. The city, which had been only a storybook place until now, was finally a reality. Flying over Paris for what seemed a long time to Orly Field gave us a chance to see what an immense city it is.

When the C−47 landed, the transportation to take us to our new quarters had not arrived, so there was time to roam around the modern airport. It was obvious that this was a hub of air travel in and out of Paris. With nothing to do but look around, we searched every corner of the airport. In a watchman's shack, we found a bronze bust of Adolf Hitler two feet high. A closer look showed a bullet hole just above its left eye, shot in anger to show the contempt the French had for him.

Eventually the trucks arrived to deliver us to a large three story school on Bessieres Boulevard, on the northern perimeter of Paris.

Paris had been liberated only a short while, and replacement troops from both the Army and Air Force were sent to Paris to be forwarded to their respective outfits.

When we were herded into the building the rooms overflowed with men. The only space for us was in the halls where cots were lined, head–to–foot, on both walls of the hallways. We had been in so many new and unusual situations in the past few months that any new one was accepted without question. Anyhow, this was only temporary and was just another stop on the way to the 404th. But we were comforted by the fact that the nine of us were still together.

Friday 29 September 1944

After checking out of our quarters, three of us, trying to get the most out of our brief layover in Paris, were roaming the streets. It was lunchtime and we had been told of an officers' club where officers of all Allied Forces were welcome as guests, so we walked in and had lunch. While there we met three American civilian girls employed as office personnel, and made arrangements to pick them up at their hotel after their work.

It had been a long, long time since we had dated American girls and this seemed like a stroke of good luck, being able to speak in our native tongue without groping for the right words. In trying to speak French, I sometimes used a word that was correct in English, but gave an altogether different meaning in French. The meaning was usually conveyed, even if the words came out wrong. Now we could communicate with these American girls without an interpreter.

We would have to be more careful, however, in the language we used. Profanity came so easily among all–male companions and natives who couldn't understand English. Sully and I could work out this problem, but profanity was so much a part of Robin's everyday conversation and was so natural that, even if he did slip, we would not have recognized it as profanity. It seems crazy to tell it, but he made it sound almost poetic.

That was a small problem at this time and we looked forward to being with someone who understood good old American. We made the dates and left for our sight–seeing, all the while discussing our new–found friends.

Some of us had dated British and French girls and in comparing the uninhibited nature of the native girls, we discussed which type we would rather be with. The more we discussed this comparison, the more we agreed that we would have more fun with the natives. So when the time drew closer to meet the girls at their hotel, our discussions turned from comparing the merits of American girls versus British and French girls to whether or not we wanted to keep our dates. The arguments were still in progress as we reached the hotel.

Upon entering the lobby, we called the girls' room to tell them we had arrived, and they said they would be right down. While waiting for them, our committee of three went outside to decide whether to keep the dates or take our chances in finding some fun—loving mademoiselles.

We could see the ornate wrought iron open—cage elevator ascend from the lobby to pick up the girls. A minute or so later the exposed cables stopped long enough for passengers to board, then the cables began moving in the opposite direction, bringing the elevator down. The committee was still in conference trying to decide whether to stay or leave.

Looking in from outside the building through the large glass windows into the lobby we could see the slow moving elevator come into view, then through the wrought iron cage, the girls' legs could be seen. At that moment, our discussions suddenly stopped and, without taking a poll, we dashed around the corner and ran away down the street, not stopping until we felt safe, several blocks away. We never got around to going to that officers' club again.

It was a cruel, mean trick to play on anyone, but each time we told it, it got funnier.

Sunday 1 October 1944

We had been in Paris enjoying the sights and everything else new to us Americans far away from home. Paris, by reputation, was a happy city, and the Lido Club and the Folies Bergere where the mademoiselles wore only G—strings and smiles were early visits for us. We were told that some of the clubs and bistros had nude waitresses, and that the Sphinx Club at 69 Rue Pigalle was such a club. We had to see this, so five of us, armed with .45 automatic pistols in shoulder holsters, left for downtown on foot since the Metros did not run on Sundays.

Five miles later when we arrived in the Monmartre district we walked up and down the streets hunting for 69 Rue Pigalle. When located, it was discovered that there was no such place as the Sphinx, so we continued, knowing that there just had to be a club like we were hunting. About five hours later, after stopping in several bistros along the way, we decided that the five miles back to our school house home would take us a long time to walk, so we headed back.

In Paris, as in Britain, all windows and doors were blacked out after dark to prevent light from shining through, making a target for enemy aircraft that might be flying over. Before getting out of Monmartre we noticed a door with a border of light around it, indicating a place of business. At this time of night, the only place of business open would be a bar, so we went in for a nightcap before tackling the long trip back to our temporary home.

Through the door was a very small room with only six small tables around which chairs were crowded. Noticeable was the difference in the intimacy between patrons of American bars and French bistros. Frenchmen seemed to be less inhibited, and the nearness of the tables guaranteed intimacy, wanted or not.

The room was filled with people having a good time, and *voila!* two waitresses, one clad in only an open–front bolero top covering her shoulders and back, and the front wide open. The other wore only a knee–length skirt, slit in the front from the waist to the hem. Nothing else. We had walked over five miles into town and another five miles looking for this very sight, and had found this small place only by accident.

Mission accomplished, and after a few minutes here, the five mile walk back to our quarters seemed insignificant as the events of the day were reviewed.

Monday 2 October 1944

With the cots so close together in head–to–foot position, and no space for storage, our bags with everything we owned were placed under the cots. At the end of the day, my pants and shirt hung at the foot of the bed. My first action each morning was to reach for the pants, slip into them and get on with the rest of the day.

Early in the morning I was awakened by a loud voice complaining that his pants were missing. Another voice announced the same thing, so I reached down to the foot of my cot to see if mine were still there. Mine were gone too.

After a few minutes of confusion it was confirmed that they were indeed stolen and not misplaced. Soon, a dozen or so of the unlucky ones, clad in only undershorts and dress shirts marched from our building through the cold open courtyard to the adjutant's office to report the theft. It was both humiliating and cold walking past the jeers and laughter of the lucky ones.

When we arrived at the office the stolen clothing had been found in a pile in the courtyard with the money gone. This was the second time I had been robbed in the service. The first time was in California two years earlier, and I attributed that theft to the lone bad apple, and continued to trust my fellow serviceman. I had learned in the past three years to trust anyone who shared the fraternity of the Air Force. Today my faith was shaken, but I couldn't help thinking that this was just another lone bad apple.

Tuesday 3 October 1944

Having been in Paris several days, we had seen first hand the sights we had only read about: public bath houses with separate stalls, sidewalk relief stations (in Oklahoma, they were called outhouses) on street corners and Parisians with few inhibitions. If they were not happy under German rule, they quickly bounced back to their free – spirit manners.

Parts of Paris, however, were still held by pockets of German resistance, and gunfire was heard occasionally. A few nights before we arrived, an American MP guarding the building we were quartered in, was injured by sniper's gunfire. For this reason, traveling in groups and carrying side arms when leaving quarters was the order of the day.

And now, to continue our sightseeing of Paris, and having nothing else to do but answer roll call, Sully, Robin and I went to the Montmartre district where the bars and girls were. As conquering heros in a liberated land the Allies were treated with admiration, respect and awe by the local citizens, and they could not do enough for us.

Women were openly suggestive with their compliments. People on the streets threw kisses our way. We were made to feel important and appreciated in Paris, even though we had never been in combat and didn't deserve their praise.

The French people on the street showed no inhibitions in expressing their gratitude to the Allies who liberated France. However, in private dealings, their aim was to separate the "rich" Americans from their easily – gotten money.

Store keepers were at a distinct advantage in their selling techniques because they were experienced hagglers, while Americans, by custom, haggled only for used cars. I felt uncomfortable with their dual display of gratitude. Regardless of my suspicions, we accepted their show of appreciation and free drinks, and basked in this glory even though we, personally, had not done anything to liberate them.

By nightfall we had taken refuge in a nightclub in Montmartre near Place Pigalle (we pronounced it Pig–Alley). Soon after we arrived and made ourselves comfortable, a portly civilian came to our table and invited us to join his party of three couples. Although he was the only one who spoke English, we communicated with them all and had a good time.

The evening wore on and I had just completed a dance with one of our hostesses. We had returned to the table only a minute or two before a man came rushing into the cabaret and walked directly to our portly host and excitedly whispered a message to him, then left. Our host stood up and abruptly ordered us to leave the premises at once as "something" was going to happen at 11:30 and we were not to be around at that time. We left the table stunned and surprised at his complete change of attitude and started for the door.

We were not satisfied with his explanation, and I returned to ask him what the problem was. When I approached him again he acted as if he had never seen me before and ordered me out of the cabaret again, this time speaking in German. As we left, others also left. Our training didn't include this type of situation, so we decided to leave it up to the Frenchmen or Germans, or whatever they were.

We roamed Monmartre until 11:30. Then out of curiosity, we returned to the cabaret to see if we could discover what the commotion was about. It was closed and the man who was guarding the door explained that our host was a high ranking officer in the FFI, the French underground organization. He had been informed that there was to be a raid on the club to seize a collaborator who was in the club at the time and had ordered us out to protect us.

We never found out anymore about the raid, but were certain that the underground war would continue to be fought by the FFI, to search out collaborators and other enemies of the Allies.

Wednesday 4 October 1944

"He was shot up pretty bad by flak. His cylinder and engine block were cracked and one aileron shot away, but he managed to return home for a safe landing. I was coaxing and guiding him back when this gun position, possibly the same one that hit him on the way out, hit him again. There were five emplacements.

I dive – bombed them and scored direct hits with the two 500 – pounders. They'll have to replace the guns. I guess it was a foolish thing to do, but I was kind of mad."

404th pilot at interrogation

We were oblivious of the actions of the men of the 404th. They needed replacement pilots, and we were on our way, but would be a few more days before we would get there. So, after several days of roll call and prowling the streets of Paris, orders came for us to load up on the trucks to be delivered to Orley Field and board C–47s to our respective units. Lined up on the ramp at a neat forty–five degree angle was a fleet of C–47s ready to takeoff with their complement of fifteen men and baggage per plane. No more than fifteen were allowed on each plane. That was regulation.

Nineteen replacement pilots with baggage were lined up ready to board the transport aimed at the 404th Fighter Group, its destination known to the pilot but not us. The line inched up as fifteen men with baggage boarded, then a hand dropped in front of me. I was number sixteen. Behind me were Sully, Charlie and Harry.

"You four men get on the next plane."

"Where is it going?"

"I don't know," the soldier at the end of the hand replied, "but you can't get on this plane. Only fifteen men and baggage are allowed on a C–47. GI regulations."

Oh, what the hell! They couldn't court martial us for following orders, so we boarded the next plane, having no idea what its destination would be.

Gosselies, Belgium is a small village situated about 30 kilometers from the French border and about 60 kilometers from our then unknown destination, St. Trond, Belgium, home of the 404th.

After the C–47 dropped us off at the airstrip, we walked into the operations shack. There we greeted the operations officer by announcing that we were assigned to the 404th, and would he please send us there. He looked at his wall map and told us that all the units in the ETO (European Theater of Operations) were changing locations so fast that he didn't know where it was. But for now, we were to go into Gosselies and stay at this little three–story walkup hotel owned and managed by Monsieur Jean and his wife, and he would send for us when he located the 404th.

It is the conquering military's privilege and duty to commandeer for their use any real estate, rolling stock, animals or people to further the cause of the war effort. M. Jean's hotel qualified under these rules, and the military had taken it over and retained M. Jean and Mme. to operate it. The operations officer assigned a driver to deliver us to the hotel and be left there until he would call us when he found our unit.

As we went into the small entry that served as a lobby, we greeted two GIs and two Belgian girls warming themselves around a small coal burner in the lobby. M. Jean and his wife accepted us as their guests and showed us to our private rooms. Charlie and I carried our gear up a narrow, steep stairway to our comfortable rooms on the third floor, and Sully and Harry were on the floor beneath us.

M. Jean was a typical gracious European maitre d' type host, complete with pencil moustache, wringing hands, bowing from the waist and clicking his heels in a salute. Everything we thanked him for was answered with "Oh NO, M'sieu, I thank YOU!" Even our cigarettes were lighted for us. M. Jean's wife (we never learned her first name) was simply Madame to us, and was a pleasant woman, short and plump. Very efficient, she took pride in her profession and made it very clear that she was not a domestic, but our hostess during our stay.

The two girls were still sitting around the table in the lobby when we came down to survey our situation. Immediately upon seeing the four of us, the two English – speaking Belgian girls turned their attention toward us. The girls seemed eager to meet us, so we became friends.

Thursday 5 October 1944

Food was always a problem in a war – ravaged land, so we had to make arrangements. We had a pretty good thing going for us and didn't want to rock the boat by showing our faces to the operations officer at the airstrip asking for food. We arranged to go to the Quartermaster of the airstrip and requisition some ten – in – one rations to take back to the hotel. Our hosts would prepare it for us, keeping some for themselves. A box of ten – in – one rations contained assorted canned foods and cigarettes, supposedly enough for ten men for one day. (Or is it one man for ten days?)

We went to the Quartermaster's shack, talked with the sergeant, and returned with two cases of ten – in – one rations. Everything went off without a hitch and the ops officer didn't know we were around. We were supplied for another two or three days. The food was shared with M. Jean and Mme. as their meager rations were precious. For us to have G.I. rations presented in such grand manner was like being served gourmet meals.

Friday 6 October 1944

Down the street from the hotel was a small bar where we went to pass the time away. Each time we were there we noticed a man who always seemed to have his share of cognac and was well on his way to becoming drunk. We supposed he was one of the regulars.

After awhile seeing him in the bar, the "drunk" came to our table stone sober and started a conversation in French with the girls. I caught a few words but the pace of speech was too fast for me. It was obvious, however, that they were discussing *"les Americains."* Translating the conversation to us, the girls told us that he was a member of the FFI, the French underground, dedicated to fight the Germans during their occupation of Belgium.

The FFI's work was risky business and very dangerous. They fought as civilians and were not protected by the international war laws covering uniformed military personnel. Their penalty, if captured, was death, most often immediately. As new soldiers who had not yet seen combat, but knew the reputation of the FFI, we respected this hero in civilian clothes.

He had checked us out before being convinced that we were really allies, and the girls were not collaborators. From then on we became good friends despite his inability to speak English.

Saturday 7 October 1944

Next day, our newly–made friend, I'll call Henri, invited us to go with him to a friend's home for supper that night and made arrangements to meet us at our hotel just before dark to take us there. He came when he promised, and the four Americans, two Belgians and the FFI started down the narrow winding streets of Gosselies. It was soon so dark that we could hardly see each other. We stayed together by the sound of our voices and holding hands in a snake line when necessary.

Gosselies seemed much larger as we snaked through the cobblestone streets, but finally we got to the outskirts of town and into cultivated fields. From there we walked in a single file on a narrow path with boards laid down where the path was too muddy to cross. Henri led the line as we all held hands in the dark field.

Seven of us in almost total darkness, four of whom where in a strange country in an unknown village going to a blacked-out house with newly-made friends made us wonder aloud if this was a trap for us to be ambushed.

As we discussed our fears, Henri announced that we had arrived. He knocked on the door and it opened a tiny bit, revealing total darkness inside. Seeing who it was, it opened wide and we accepted our guests' invitation to *"entrez"* into the darkened house, praying we were wrong about the ambush. When the seven of us got inside, the door was sealed against escaping light, and our hosts turned on the lights. We were safe inside and among friends.

A middle-aged man and his wife were genuinely honored to have Americans share their home this evening. With great hospitality, they served us a well-prepared meal of *"hos und pfeffer."*

Neither our hosts nor Henri spoke any English, but there was no misunderstanding the spirit of the visit that evening, shared by allies with much respect for one another. We Americans were honored because we were accepted by our gracious host and hostess and the member of the FFI. They felt honored by serving members of the liberating army who would leave their homeland to help others in another part of the world.

When it was time to leave, our FFI guide led us back to M. Jean's hotel and said goodbye and we never saw him again.

Monday 9 October 1944

After five lost days and nights in Gosselies, we decided that the 404th FG was wondering what had happened to their lost replacement pilots. So we went back to the base operations officer to see if he had located our unit yet. He had forgotten all about us, but made a phone call and located our outfit and was told that they were indeed interested in our whereabouts. He made arrangements to have a truck pick us up the next morning and deliver us to St. Trond.

CHANDELLE

CHAPTER FIVE

ARRIVAL IN COMBAT

Wednesday 11 October 1944

Our arrival at the 404th FG near St. Trond, Belgium followed the group's arrival by only a short time. Activity was bustling, setting up operations and digging in for a winter's stay. The group had hopped, skipped and jumped from one airstrip to another since D – Day, trying to keep up with our infantry and tanks on their march through France and into Belgium.

The 404th had covered 600 miles in one month by the time Sully, Charlie, Harry and I had caught up with them. When we arrived, Harry and Charlie had already been assigned to the 506th Squadron and Sully and I to the 508th.

Squadrons were housed in separate buildings, the 508th in a large building we called the "chateau," a former Luftwaffe pilots quarters. Although not a castle as chateaux were depicted in my old geography books, it was a large comfortable brick building with electricity, running water and inside baths. The bedrooms were large enough to crowd four or five men into.

Because it was newly occupied by the squadron, men were housed in rooms on a first come – first served basis. Sully and I were late arriving and temporarily bunked with a couple of men in the attic until we could find a room together. Within a couple of days, the chateau felt like home and being with a permanent organization made us part of a family.

The "Chateau" at A-92 near St. Trond, Belgium, home of the 404th Fighter Group for seven months.

St. Trond is 37 miles from Aachen, the first city in Germany the Allies planned to take. The Germans were defending it with all their might to prevent the Allies from setting foot on their homeland.

The march through Europe would be slowing down for awhile, now that winter was coming and there would be fewer flying days to help the ground troops. Besides, the Germans were fighting harder on their home field.

The ready room, conveniently located adjacent to the hangars, was being built from the ground up. With pride of ownership, we all pitched in to make it as comfortable as possible, since most of our non-flying time would be spent in it. That was where we held briefings before missions and interrogations afterwards, and waited for the missions we were not on to come in. A small snack bar was built in one corner of the room, and tables were found or built on which to play cards, read or write letters home.

Dishes, cooking utensils, glasses and silverware to stock the snack bar were being scrounged from anyplace we could get them. It was about this time "Buzz Boy" was shot down on a mission about fifty miles inside the enemy lines. For three days we had no idea what had happened to him, and had given up hope of ever seeing him again.

Members of the 508th Fighter Squadron in the ready room relaxing between missions. Their clothing indicates they were not scheduled for one, otherwise they would be in flying suits.

He had bailed out but was not injured nor discovered by the enemy, we learned later. Leaving his plane and hiding his parachute, he traveled by night and hid by day. He stayed as far from the main roads as possible and always moved west. He was helped by friendly German farmers who gave him food and hid him when German soldiers came near.

Determined to make it back to the base, he crossed the Meuse River at night and eventually arrived back home three days later with enough silverware stuffed in his pockets to add to the snack bar.

Thursday 19 October 1944

The group had been at A–92 (airfields were identified by letters and numbers) only about three weeks and was getting settled, as we expected to stay here during the winter. Besides, regular missions had to be flown as this was our reason for being here. I had not flown my first mission yet, and was not due for one today, and was beginning to wonder when I would get my chance. I would find out in a few minutes.

The scheduled missions were delayed due to a low overcast with no promise of the weather improving soon, so it was not certain that any would go out today. Nevertheless, Colonel Moon decided to make a weather reconnaissance across the line to see if a limited mission could be flown.

Squadron Commander (later Group Commander) Leo C. Moon was a tough, well–respected leader, and an excellent pilot. He believed he was sent here to fly and do the best he could in his job and never missed an opportunity to fly. He would hand–pick a wingman, and the two of them go on a search–and–destroy mission when the rest of the group was grounded due to the weather. He was looking for a reason to fly today and found one.

Looking at the schedule on the board and not finding my name on it, he told me to go to a plane he had already assigned for his wingman, and we would fly a weather recon. He briefed me on what we would do and how it would be done, and admonished me not to lose him in the overcast. This would be my first combat flight.

A low overcast was not my first choice of weather to fly my first mission in, but instrument flying was a large part of flying training and I was confident in it, so off we went.

I didn't fear the enemy because I didn't know what to expect, and Jerry wasn't likely to be out in this overcast. Besides, we were going to cross the line only a short distance into enemy territory and return home. I wasn't nervous, but was apprehensive because this would be my first mission. When Colonel Moon picked me to go with him I looked forward to getting my first mission in the record book.

Mission Number One was uneventful. Flying low under the overcast at no more than 500 feet and crossing over into enemy territory, we found that the weather was so bad that all the flying was called off for the rest of the day. There was no flak and no activity of any kind when we crossed the bomb line. The weather was noted and we returned to the base.

It seemed like an easy mission to me, but when I crossed into enemy territory for the first time I got the sensation of being in a forbidden place. If this was all there was to combat flying, the others would be no sweat. I had a lot to learn. It wasn't all like this. But Mission Number One was accomplished, and I was ready for more.

Friday 20 October 1944
The ever–changing situations of war also changed the use of the fighter–bombers. Before D–Day, the P–47, as well as all other

fighters stationed in England, were used extensively for escort of medium and heavy bombers in addition to dive bombing, and often resulted in air–to–air combat because the Luftwaffe was more in evidence then. After D–Day, the P–47 was primarily used as a fighter–bomber because of its ability to carry heavy loads of armament and take a lot of punishment, but air–to–air encounters also occurred though not as frequently.

Now that the Allies were on the Continent, fighter groups were stationed there to be closer to the ground troops they were to support, and to disrupt the enemy's movement of supplies and troops. The Allies had air superiority, and German fighters usually steered clear of large numbers of Allied fighters. After arriving on the Continent, the 404th Fighter Group, if not all other P–47 groups on the Continent, was used almost exclusively as fighter–bombers.

The 404th, The Tin Hornets, was made up of three squadrons, each with its identifying name: the 506th Squadron, Pintail; 507th, Crocus; and the 508th, Granite. When on missions, squadrons were usually comprised of either three or four flights of four planes per flight, but the squadron commander could change the formation any way he needed to. Single flights of four planes or even an odd number of planes occasionally went out when the mission called for it. The formation of a squadron or group mission was made to fit the situation.

Identity by name was important and a single aircraft in any of the three squadrons could be quickly identified by its position in the group. The first flight of each squadron was Red Flight, the second, White Flight and the third, Blue Flight. If there was a fourth it would be Yellow Flight. Individual planes in each flight were numbered One, Two, Three and Four, so it was easy to identify the third plane in the second flight in the 508th Squadron by calling Granite White Three.

The last plane in the squadron or group was jokingly (though seldom funny) called Purple Heart Corner or Tail–end Charlie, but only on the ground. In the air, it was serious and he was called by his position. Dodging flak was no fun so if a position was called to be warned about a bandit or a gun emplacement on the ground, the one warned had better know who he was.

In the heat of battle, if he knew his buddy's plane by the number on its side, it would be more personal and might get his attention quicker to holler, "Sully, bandit at five o'clock high!"

FORMATION FLYING

INSTRUMENT (OR SHOW)

When going through an overcast, the leader flies on instruments and the other planes fly by visual reference to him. This formation requires full concentration and reliance on the leader. It is also used for show or pass in review.

BASIC COMBAT

This is a loose formation that provides excellent visibility and mutual tail cover. It is simple, fluid and can be adapted to any combat grouping.

SQUADRON BOX

RED FLIGHT

WHITE FLIGHT

BLUE FLIGHT

YELLOW FLIGHT

This combines the Basic Combat flights into one squadron of three or four flights. It has the same advantages as the Basic Combat and can be quickly separated into individual flights.

Descriptive words, phrases and expressions coined for special situations became a natural part of conversation. "Big Friend" and "Little Friend" were easily understood as Allied bomber and Allied fighter. "Bandits," obviously, were enemy planes while a "Bogey" was an unknown aircraft. "Targets of opportunity," "Armed recon," "Bought the farm," "Fat, dumb and happy" and other phrases were short, expressive and universal among Air Force personnel.

A P–47D–30, Sweet Music, shows off its artwork on its fuselage.

Some words such as "radar" and "snafu" are acronyms and have become part of the English language, defined in the dictionary. "flak" comes from the German word *fliegerabwherkanone.*

Airplanes, too, were often named by the pilot or crew chief to whom they were assigned. The names had personal meaning to these men. "Pride 'O Dogpatch" could have been "Pappy Yocum's plane, and "Immanuel" had a religious connotation. You didn't have to guess what "Flak Valley Express" meant. "I'll Get By," a popular song title, expressed the confidence of Group Commander Colonel Moon. Others were "Pretty Baby," "Maggie Zass," "Lo Flow," "Sweet Music," and many others.

Nicknames of the men also played an important part of our lives while living together. Sully called Ed "Cooner" because he thought Ed looked like a raccoon as he silently peered down from his upper bunk at the other roommates. "Pappy" Yocum was obviously named for one of Al Capp's "Li'l Abner" cartoon characters. Why "Buckshot" was so named was a mystery to me but was as natural as calling the P–47 the Jug. My name became "Kay" for brevity and because few people can look at it and pronounce it.

Sully, however, called me "Kayho," from a private joke. Our pug–nosed Irish squadron commander insisted on being called "Kelly" when in private conversation with those close to him.

Our group commander was called "Little Caesar," and "Senator" was so–called because of his handlebar moustache, caricatured by so many cartoonists. Not everyone had a nickname, but one could be counted on if someone had special features like short and round, like "Beaucoup". After being called by a nickname for so long, a man hardly answered to his real name, and few of the others even knew his real one. For some reason, a person felt that he belonged to a group if he was liked well enough to be given a nickname.

Saturday 21 October 1944

Now that the group had settled at its new base, an attempt was made to have a regular flying schedule with some days off: fly twelve and off two. The weather changed constantly from flying to non–flying and replacement pilots came in. High mission pilots went back home and, with other uncertainties, it was a short–lived schedule. Pilots took advantage of it while it lasted, however, and were allowed to go for two days anyplace they could walk or hitchhike.

The Battle of Aachen, the first major battle in Germany, was taking place at this time. Pilots seeing the war from only the air would have an opportunity to go to Aachen and see it from another perspective. The contrast between our comfortable brick chateau with electricity, running water and a fireplace would be like going camping, we thought.

Transportation was not too hard to come by, so on our off duty days, four of us took a jeep to Aachen to spend the night with the foot soldiers. We didn't know what to expect when we got there, but whatever it was, we were not quite prepared for it. When we returned, our respect for the ground pounders had grown by leaps and bounds.

We, too, had been initiated into tent cities with mud floors and no heat. "C" rations and "K" rations had often been our menu before being sent to St. Trond. Hot meals from mess kits were also appreciated in our travels, but at no time during our mud floor and "C" ration days were we ever shot at by the enemy while on the ground.

We headed east into the unknown, to explore another way of life. Men who had already gone to Aachen advised us not to overlook a large country home just inside Germany, only a few kilometers behind the Siegfried Line.

The Seigfried Line, built in the 1930's to defend the German border, was a series of barriers close together to prevent tanks from rolling over them. A formidable sight at one time, it had outlived its usefulness, what with more modern warfare. The road crossing from Belgium into Germany at that point was situated where barriers had been removed to make room for a road, making passage possible.

Just beyond the Siegfried Line, nestled in the beautiful forest surrounding it, we found the once well–maintained home. The occupants had hurriedly vacated it just before the Americans had overtaken this area only a few days earlier, leaving much of the furnishings still inside.

The respect we had for the property of others suddenly evaporated and was replaced by our curiosity at the moment. After a hasty tour around the house, we entered to find a partially furnished home with some crystal and china still in place. There was no doubt that people of means and good taste had occupied this house.

Roaming through the house without an invitation, we felt like the trespassers we were. Being uninvited in a private home, it would not have surprised us if the owner had barged in and demanded that we explain what we were doing in his home. We made visual note of the furnishings, commenting that it would be nice to take some for souvenirs, but went on our way empty–handed.

It was mid–afternoon when we arrived in Aachen, and the infantry wondered why we chose to come to a hell hole like this. They had been fighting for several days without relief and it was neither pleasant nor safe. The Germans still held the hill facing the main street of town with a perfect view of everything that went on in the street. Simply crossing the street made the Americans vulnerable to sniper fire.

The infantry greeted us as allies and were cordial, but continued doing business as usual during our stay. After settling us in the basement of a bombed out building, a soldier pointed to a crudely–painted sign at the end of the street that announced "Don't go beyond this point! The enemy is 200 yards away! Are you crazy?" Our orientation was to read the sign.

A bed for the night was a space in the corner of the basement floor of a bombed out building where the debris had been moved to one side. Trying to sleep leaning against a wall with no cover except a heavy flying suit didn't strike me as a pleasant way to spend a weekend. I remembered the sign at the end of the street and mentally answered its question, "Maybe I am."

Next morning, after a fitful night of wondering if the next shell had our names on it, we decided that we should get the hell out of the foot soldiers' way and let them do their job. An informal poll of the fly–boys showed that we would rather be shot at in the sky than on the ground, so we headed back to our steam–heated chateau with the inside toilet.

On our return trip, we again passed the large home we had inspected going to Aachen, and glanced that way and longed for some keepsake from the house. A jeep with four men and a few belongings didn't leave much room for extra baggage, so we continued for home.

Saturday 28 October 1944

My first mission gave me credit for having been in combat, though not literally true. Crossing the bomb line gave the qualification, but there was no action. When my second mission was scheduled, I was ready, eager and able to go. I had sat with other pilots as they were briefed, and was an experienced listener. Now it would be my turn to act.

I had practiced in my mind going to the plane, taxiing to the runway, taking off and joining the squadron in the air to head into enemy territory. There my dreaming stopped because I didn't know what would happen after that.

The second mission began as I thought it would. After the join–up and climb to 10,000 feet, it was a serene flight above the wispy white clouds. The sun shone brightly and occasionally flashed off the silver wings of the neighboring planes and I was oblivious of the fighting on the ground ahead and below. It was a nice flight.

Liege was sighted below us and soon we would cross into enemy territory on our way to the target east of Aachen. The squadron passed over the invisible bomb line. I was aware that we were over enemy ground, but there was no sensation of foreboding as on the first mission.

Flak was not encountered immediately after crossing the bomb line, but as the squadron headed toward Aachen, it could be seen in the distance. There were black puffs of smoke, all about the same level, with airplanes flying through them, seemingly without concern. It didn't look dangerous to me. Movies were shown in training and explanations were given of flak, what it looked like and how to evade it. Upon my seeing the first bursts of actual flak that, until now had been only in films, I thought, "that's just like in the movies."

The squadron had begun flak evasion, changing direction periodically so as not to give the enemy ground gunners the opportunity to track our path with radar. As we neared the target east of Aachen, flak became more intense until some of the planes were bounced around by the impact of near misses. My first near miss initiated me into a real combat situation and proved I was wrong – it was not at all like in the movies.

The squadron broke up into separate flights and strafed and dropped bombs on the trucks and tanks on the road to Aachen. It was a short distance of about seventy – five miles. The mission was over within an hour, so the squadron leader gathered his birds and returned to base without a loss.

With Mission Number Two completed, I felt I had really been initiated. Another mission on the same day, and I was now a three – mission experienced pilot.

Sunday 29 October 1944

The ratio of pilots to aircraft was never one – to – one. There were always more pilots, therefore not all of them had aircraft assigned to them to call "my airplane." Aircraft were assigned to pilots by seniority, so when a new man came in he flew a P – 47 assigned to another pilot who would not be flying that mission. The new man seldom flew the same P – 47 regularly. This didn't cause any problems but everyone looked forward to having a Jug he could call his own, even if he had to share it with someone else.

One of the privileges that went with having one's own airplane was that the pilot could have his name painted on the side and his very own art painted on the plane.

His responsibility was to see that it was properly maintained. That was no problem, either, because every P – 47 had its own crew chief and armorer, each with his crew. The armorer was responsible for attaching the bombs and rockets on the wings and belly as well as the external fuel tanks. He made sure the eight .50 caliber guns were aimed right and shot when they were supposed to; that the bombs dropped when they ought to; that the proper rockets were attached and all the other things pertaining to armament operated as they should.

The crew chief was in charge of everything on his plane; had to know every nut and bolt in it, and make sure his crew did its job well. The P – 47 was the crew chief's airplane even more than it was the pilot's. He went to bed with it and got up with it, fed it, nurtured it and breathed life into it in the wee hours of the morning so it would be ready to fly on the first morning mission.

The author and his crew chief, Melvin Houston, also from Oklahoma.

The crew chief's word was virtually the final one as to whether the plane would fly or not, not the pilot's. Maintenance of aircraft in our group was better than it was in training in the States. Consequently, confidence in the maintenance was great and the relationship between the pilot and his crew chief was a very close one.

When my name went up on the scheduling board with the assignment of the plane I would fly, I never gave it a thought that the plane would not be warmed up and ready to fly when I got to it. It might have been on a mission the day before and come back with flak damage, the radio out or any number of things wrong with it. The ground crew worked hard and long to get it ready for me, sometimes far into the night and up early the next morning. The crew chief and his crew were as anxious as the pilot for it to come back in good condition.

The armorer who saw that the ammo bays were filled and the bombs were hung properly took great pains to make sure everything was in top shape. The parachute rigger and all others readying the plane for missions were links in a strong chain, any of which could fail in its job and cause a disaster. Occasionally there would be an abortion of a plane on a mission for failure of equipment, usually very minor, but I always took off with full confidence in my equipment. So while the pilot was the captain of the ship and was responsible for everything about it, as a practical matter, he had very little to be concerned about. The crew chief and armorer and their crews performed their duties efficiently.

All P–47s were not alike. There were actually over 50 different models, from the XP–47B, the first experimental one, to the P–47N20, the last one made. Additionally, some were modified in the field to some degree, though not designated as different models. For instance, the group commander had his eight guns rigged to fire only four at a time, thus getting twice as much strafing time as the rest of us whose eight guns fired simultaneously. Targets varied and four guns were plenty of firepower for some, while larger ones required the full firepower of all eight.

Armorers loading belts of ammunition in the wings and cleaning the bores of the four machine guns. Note that only three of the wing–mounted guns are visible. The fourth is flush with the leading edge of the wing and not noticable. (U.S.A.F.)

Imagine the poor replacement pilot coming fresh from the States and having to get checked out in the type of aircraft he already had high time in. Actually the transition from one model to another was not drastic, and simply being told the difference usually sufficed for his check – out.

The method of releasing bombs or external fuel tanks varied on some models, and the release handles were sometimes in a slightly different position. Anything attached to the wings or belly could be released one at a time or all at once. The selection of the bomb or bombs to be dropped was accomplished by different switches or levers, also depending on models of planes. In addition, bombs were to be armed before a run, otherwise they would not explode on impact. It was a safety factor to prevent accidents when necessary to land with bombs attached. It didn't always work that way, but the chances of such an accident were rare. Men who had had an attached bomb drop off in landing and explode after tumbling end – over – end down the runway wouldn't agree that the accidents were rare.

Arming the bomb was accomplished with another control allowing a small propeller on the nose of the bomb to turn in the wind. The bomb would then explode on impact after the prop made a specific number of turns.

We were carrying two 500 – lb bombs on the wings and a 260 – lb fragmentation anti – personnel bomb on the belly on my fourth mission, and I was assigned someone else's plane. The group arrived over the target and orders were given to select the two wing bombs. That would make the plane 1,000 pounds lighter before making another pass to drop the belly bomb. Dropping the wing bombs first would keep the plane in balance and make it more maneuverable for subsequent passes.

The right and left bombs were selected and armed, and I entered the dive. At the drop point, I released the selected bombs and began a pull – up in a steep climb. The center one was not to be dropped until the next pass. When the bombs dropped, my plane lurched hard to the right and the right wing became heavier than the left. I knew I had not been hit by flak but I couldn't figure it out, so I climbed back to altitude with the squadron for the belly bomb drop.

As we circled for the second pass, I heard a voice on the radio calling. "Granite Blue Two, you still have your right wing bomb." I had a bomb still attached! I was new in combat on only my fourth mission, and this had not happened to me before, although some of the others had come back and landed with their bombs still attached.

I now knew why the right wing seemed heavy. I pulled the right selection handle again, thinking that the pin holding the bomb had not traveled far enough to release it, but nothing happened. I couldn't go down to drop the belly bomb with the right wing still holding the 500–pounder, so I circled until the others finished the job without me. All this time I tugged and pulled the right handle trying to disengage the missile with no results.

The group completed its work and headed home while I was trying to release that damned bomb. As we departed enemy territory and were over our own, the thought occurred to me that I had been pulling only on the right handle. In a test, I pulled on the left one again to compare the feel with the right one. There was no difference, which led me to believe that the center handle was for the right wing. I suddenly realized that I had not even tried to pull the center handle to drop the belly bomb, as I had not gone on the second run. It had dropped when I thought I released the right wing bomb.

I had to get rid of the 500–lb weight before landing, so I veered away from the formation and picked out a nice open field in Belgium. The bomb was jettisoned without being armed to prevent it from exploding, hoping its finder would think it was dropped at a time when this territory was in German hands. It was an embarrassing relief getting rid of this error.

In the confusion of flying a plane new to me, I had mistaken the bomb release sequence and pulled the wrong handles. Soon afterwards I was assigned my own airplane, Number 7JU, and I was never faced with this problem again.

P–47D–30–RA flown by author. Almost 16,000 P–47s were built, more than any other fighter at the time.

Thursday 9 November 1944

As mentioned earlier, there were three or four flights in a squadron, a flight being four planes. With three squadrons in the group, it would normally have from thirty–six to forty–eight planes in the group. The group or squadron commanders, however, could change this configuration any way they saw fit, depending on the mission or target.

Missions were flown as a group with one primary target or as individual squadrons with targets for each squadron. Occasionally, four–plane flights went out.

The 508th sent sixteen P–47s plus one, on a mission. The seventeenth plane was a "spare" with full combat load, and tagged along on every mission following the others to the bomb line. If any of the scheduled planes had to abort, the spare filled his slot and completed the mission with the others. If none aborted, the spare would return and not get credit for the mission.

I was spare, so when the squadron leader's wingman had a mechanical problem and returned to the base I took his place. The target was a marshalling yard at Bergheim, halfway between Julich and Cologne. As we circled over the target area planning our run, the enemy threw up colorful red and green flak designed to attract our attention long enough for their anti–aircraft guns to track us and give them a better chance to hit us. Their trick didn't work and we dived from 6,000 feet dropping our two 500–lb bombs, then returning to fire our rockets. A few strafing runs with the wing guns and we were through with that target.

Now we were scattered all over the sky. With the mission completed, all that was left to do was to get back to Belgium safely. The Senator, squadron leader on this flight, had already climbed to about 6,000 feet before he called his squadron to rendezvous. The standard procedure for a rendezvous was for the leader to circle until all planes were generally together. He flew directly toward a cloud without circling, allowing only those close enough to him to form with him. When his plane entered the dense cloud, I was the only one who caught up with him and we were flying a two–plane formation.

The ground, the horizon and the sky had all vanished and we were then in a thick white cloud flying on instruments. When in close formation, the leader navigated, and the wingman flew in direct relationship to his leader. The wingman had to make constant throttle corrections, climbing, diving and turning with the leader as one unit, doing exactly as his leader. The wingman's eyes were glued to the lead plane almost without blinking, since a fraction of a second of inattention in close formation at this speed could result in an almost certain fatal accident. The leader was trusted implicitly, and close formation flying on instruments placed two or more lives in his hands.

Although my eyes were never off the Senator's plane for one moment, even in the dense cloud, my peripheral vision caught the movement of another plane attaching itself to the Senator's left wing directly opposite my position. There were now three planes in a V formation and the cloud had completely engulfed us although visibility within the cloud had improved somewhat.

Soon another Thunderbolt appeared to form on my right wing, making a flight of four. After flying in this formation awhile I noticed the Senator's left wingman drop below and cross under us, then leave the formation. He appeared to have shot up to the right at a thirty-degree angle climb without losing any speed, even in his apparent steep climb. Something was wrong but I couldn't put my finger on it.

Next, my wingman slid away from my right wing and crossed under me to fill the place of the departed plane, and again formed a three-plane V. Shortly thereafter, the left wingman did the same as the first, and shot into the sky without losing any speed.

It was time for me to look at my instruments for guidance. With planned caution I stole enough half-second glances at my instruments to tell me that we were exceeding normal cruising speed by quite a bit and were in an approximate thirty-degree diving bank to the left. My only thought at this moment was for self-preservation, and my next reaction was the same as the others who had left the formation. I pulled up to straight and level flight away from the Senator, calling for him to do the same, but received no answer.

Alone and lost, as the navigation was left to my leader, and flying instruments over enemy territory, my immediate thoughts were: Radar! The Germans could easily track me with their radar if I flew straight and level. It was easier to fly instruments straight and level than to fly erratically for flak evasion. I wondered what the terrain elevation was here in enemy territory. Were there any mountains? These questions needed to be answered for my peace of mind.

The best advice in flying school was "Don't panic," and that was the time to practice the advice, so I settled down to assess my situation and estimate my general position. Since the bomb line ran generally north and south, and deeper into Germany was east, my decision to head west was easy to make. Climbing to get over any mountains that might be in the way, I decided that flak evasion wasn't that much trouble after all, even on instruments. The alternative could be unpleasant.

Almost safe now that I had passed this crisis, I turned my thoughts to the Senator and his safety. What happened to him? Did he finally see his predicament and pull up as we had done? I would find out when I returned to the base, so I continued my flight back wondering about him. He had already narrowly escaped death when he rode his plane down in a belly landing in Normandy during the June invasion of France. Would his good luck hold out?

A short flight can seem like an eternity when alone over enemy territory, but friendly territory came into view and my mission was over.

After the interrogation, we waited and hoped he would come straggling in as so many others had done. By the time we calculated that his fuel would be gone we gave up hope. Later, when the land he was flying over was taken by the Allies, his calculated path of flight was traced and the ground searched without a trace or clue of his whereabouts. He was listed as Missing In Action.

Saturday 11 November 1944

It was ironical that this was Armistice Day, celebrating the end of World War One, twenty–six years earlier. Nevertheless, this war continued without recognition, and the only celebration was the unwitting "bombs bursting in air."

All of our missions had the same format: briefing, fly out, hit the target, come home to interrogation and critique. More specifically, we assembled in the briefing room where the mission leader pointed to the map with its heavy black bomb line and the big red blotches denoting heavy flak pockets. He briefed his pilots on the target and showed the route to be taken. The squadron would dog–leg around heavy flak concentrations, especially at Bonn and Cologne. The direction of attack and how long the mission would be was explained.

We were told of weather conditions expected and the type of bombs and whether external fuel tanks would be used. The return course back home and all other pertinent information were discussed. Photographs of the target and surrounding landmarks were shown to familiarize us with their appearances.

Flights (or squadrons, if it was a group mission) were assigned to different levels when at the target. Watches were synchronized and the start–engine and takeoff times were given. Pilots then picked up their parachutes and went out to their planes.

A .45 caliber automatic pistol carried in a shoulder holster and an escape kit were permanently issued. The escape kit was a clear plastic box about six inches by four inches and contained matches, compass, adhesive tape and bandage. Included were a small hacksaw blade, tablets to sterilize water for drinking, two ounces of chocolate, a hypodermic needle and container of morphine. Pictures of the pilot in civilian clothes were carried in case fake papers were needed to be made in the event of a bail out. Pilots also carried a small amount of German money and a few other small useful items.

When I was scheduled for a mission, there was always a fleeting thought about whether this would be my day to "buy the farm." Seldom persisting, it lasted only until the briefing. I realized that the attention I gave at the briefing would have a direct bearing on my performance during the mission, so I tried to understand every detail.

After the briefing and during my walk to the plane, my thoughts were a mixture of anticipation, a little fear, a silent plea to God and review of the briefing. As soon as I was strapped in the cockpit all these thoughts were replaced by the mechanics of starting the plane and taxiing and taking off, keeping it straight down the runway, wheels up, correct airspeed and throttle, finding my leader, close formation, instruments and a thousand and one other details. In general, flying the airplane. Fear was seldom on my mind once in the cockpit as there were too many other things to be concerned about.

There were reasons for aborting a mission, both justified and imagined. Aborting was far from my mind but for some reason I felt uneasy about this one and I didn't know why. The uneasiness persisted during the climb to altitude and on through the clouds to 12,000 feet. I knew the bomb line would be reached soon, and also knew there was a spare plane in the event of an abortion.

A pilot must keep his head "on a swivel" to know exactly where he was in relation to the other planes in the sky. He must not become hypnotized by the instruments in the cockpit or anything else that might prevent him from being aware of everything around him.

There was usually a small amount of air leaking around the seal where the canopy met the windscreen. Because of my uneasiness, every time I turned my head, the engine had a different sound, making me wonder if there was something wrong with the plane. With every movement of my head the sound got worse and I was certain something was wrong.

Approaching the bomb line, a decision had to be made whether to abort or not, and at the last minute I decided not to take a chance with the load we had, twisting, turning and diving. If something was wrong now, how would it perform during these antics? My mind was made up. I called the squadron leader and told him that my engine was running rough and I would have to abort. The spare replaced me as my request was acknowledged and I returned to the base.

During the flight back it still seemed that the plane was not operating as it ought but when the crew chief checked it over, he found nothing wrong. I thought about the events leading up to this abortion. Did I abort because I was scared? If so, why? And if so, I didn't know it. I had had missions before and, although I was apprehensive on every one of them, aborting due to fear never entered my mind. Why, then, was this one different? It was not a premonition, as we discovered at the interrogation that the mission was successful and had no problems. There was no explanation. On my next mission my reactions were back to normal as they had been before this one.

Saturday 25 November 1944

Two weeks after my first abortion, the mission had begun normally. As I was climbing for altitude, my rubber-soled boots kept slipping on the metal runs under the rudder pedals, and had no traction. Looking down I could see and smell gasoline leaking on the floor of the cockpit. I thought it was from an overflow and would soon evaporate, so I wasn't too concerned, but I thought it best to keep an eye on the developments between here and the bomb line.

The squadron was still climbing when we were about five miles from the line, and by now there was quite a lot of gasoline sloshing around on the floor. I made the decision to abort, and the spare again took my place. The leak became worse as I flew back to the base, but I landed with no problems and reported it to my crew chief, who found the problem and repaired it.

Because of our interest in the outcome of every mission, most pilots attended the interrogation, whether on the mission or not. Especially me, this time, as I had been scheduled for this one. The target was attacked and all planes returned safely. The mission went well and was considered a success.

Almost as an afterthought, the operations officer who led the mission, discussed abortions. He mentioned in his diplomatic way that there were abortions which may not have been necessary, and for us to guard against those times when one was considered for reasons other than mechanical failure.

The presence of high octane gasoline in the cockpit made this flight dangerous for me, and the abortion was justified. However, I looked back a few weeks before when I could not explain just why I returned to the base, and felt that the ops officer's discussion was intended only for me, and as a warning to the others.

Tuesday 28 November 1944

It was my second mission of the day and I was flying assistant flight leader in Elton's flight. The primary target this afternoon was a water tower atop a dam at Wipperfurth being used as an observation post and gun emplacement. The weather was clear when we arrived at our destination in the early afternoon and we could see barrage balloons over the target in the distance. They were tethered by cables just daring anyone to go beneath them. An airplane could get its wings ripped off easily by the steel cables holding the balloons, so we were careful not to give them the chance by getting too low.

Elton dived in from about 12,000, and my wingman and I followed him to bomb the observation tower. After the bomb drop we climbed back up and couldn't tell if any damage was done as the tower was still standing. We followed the leader for another strafing run, our bullets going into the single window on the side of the tower we were attacking.

Anti-aircraft fire got lighter with each pass, and after one bomb run and three strafing passes, it was so light that we fell into game-playing to see if we could deflate some balloons with our tracer bullets.

A barrage balloon makes a big target when coming in close, and we couldn't miss. It would really be something to see one of those things blow up after being hit with a tracer, but none of them were affected by our repeated passes. We tried time after time to explode the balloons, knowing they were undoubtedly filled with non-inflammable helium.

Elton could see that we were wasting our fuel and ammo with this nonsense, so he called us to rendezvous and head back to the barn.

With each pass I made, I felt that the next one would be the one that would blow the lid off and set the world afire. When Elton called for the rendezvous I called him back, "Elton, let me make one last pass! I think I can get one!"

While the squadron was rendezvousing I was circling for one last pass, and was on my run when all hell broke loose and the plane almost did a snap roll. The controls were stiff and I had to fight hard to keep it from spiraling into the ground which was coming up fast to meet me.

As I was struggling with the controls, I looked at the left wing and saw that it had got a direct hit under it. The hit opened the ammo door which was hinged from the rear on top of the wing. When the wind caught the door it was ripped from the wing and fell fluttering to earth, leaving a gaping hole with three belts of .50 caliber shells trailing out of it, flapping in the slipstream.

Luckily, the control cables were not cut, but I had a problem on my hands trying to keep the plane level. With the loss of the ammo door, the plane had lost most of the lift on that wing, so it was literally flying with one wing and a fervent prayer. After trimming the aileron all the way to compensate for loss of lift of the left wing, the Jug could be maneuvered in an acceptable manner. At the moment, any manner was acceptable.

After announcing that I was hit, I tried to climb back to the squadron, but couldn't make it. The hit had cut the lines operating the rate instruments. The airspeed and the rate-of-climb indicators were inoperative. I couldn't tell if I was climbing or not or how fast I was going. For all I knew, I could have stalled out any moment. No matter how clear the sky was, the P-47 was flown in large part by instruments, and I really missed mine then.

My wingman, Bob Hurst, quickly came to my aid and I flew on his wing back to the base. We were vulnerable to ground fire, as my plane couldn't climb with the limited lift in the left wing. We had to hold as much altitude as possible in case I had to bail out unexpectedly. Luckily we did not attract any small arms fire or heavy flak on our return. It was a welcome relief when the field came into view. The total mission was only one and one-half hours long, but the trip back home seemed like it took all day.

Bob was so intent on getting me back to the base in one piece that he didn't give any thought to the possibility that my plane could have snapped into his at any time due to my limited control. Tucked in tight on Bob's wing, he brought me in to land, calling airspeed and altitude to me as we descended in a straight-in approach. When he was sure I would not stall too high, he pulled up to let me land on my own, and he went around to make his landing.

The author, with parachute still strapped on, shortly after landing with damage to the left wing.

Having a plane bounce violently from a near miss of flak was pretty disturbing, and having a direct hit can momentarily cause panic and disorientation. My experience was reminiscent of another pilot in our squadron who was also hit in the left wing. He immediately lost control and almost flipped over, just as I had done. After regaining control he kept hearing an awful noise and thought the plane was coming apart, then he discovered he was holding his control stick with the gun trigger so tightly that he was still firing his guns all this while. He was as lucky as I was to limp back home and report it.

All's well that ends well, they say, but many times since then I have heard my own words ring in my ears, "Let me make one last pass!" It could have been my very last.

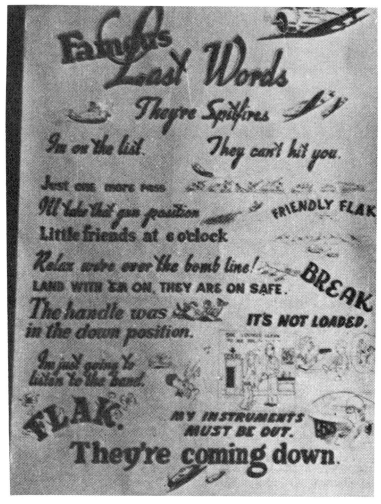

Poster reminds pilots to be alert and not fly "fat, dumb and happy."

Friday 8 December 1944

I was scheduled to fly the group commander's wing and expected it to be just another mission. I don't mean to make it sound as if all missions were alike. On the contrary, each one was unique, and yet, most of them had the same pattern: takeoff, go to the target, do the job and return home. All the while, look out for flak. If there was one common thread in almost all missions, it was flak.

The events of the day made it an unusual one, beginning before takeoff. Taxiing out to the runway took a little extra care due to the strong winds. The weather was marginal because of the crosswinds on the only runway we had, but the mission was not scrubbed. Once airborne, it would be OK, but with the two wing bombs and a 110–gallon external belly tank sloshing around, the takeoff would be tricky.

Standard procedure during a normal mission, if any could be called normal, was for the planes to takeoff by element (two planes), with the wingman to the side and slightly behind the leader. Exceptions to that required us to takeoff singly if it was deemed dangerous. For example, too heavy a load, or rough runways that had been bombed and patched, or strong crosswinds that made control of the aircraft difficult. Two of these exceptions were present.

Two P–47s takeoff in formation from A–92. Note the bombers in the background. Damaged bombers often landed at A–92 to be repaired enough to fly back to their base.

The wind was quite strong at 90 degrees from the left, and the decision whether to takeoff by element would be made by the group commander before taking off. I was pretty sure that we would takeoff individually because of the wind and heavy load. The group leader pulled up into takeoff position and I taxied in on his left wing and back a little where I could see him. I waited for his forward throttle, then I expected to push mine forward a few seconds later to takeoff singly. He looked at me and waved for me to come closer abreast of him. It seemed unusual and I wondered exactly what he meant, but I pulled up a little more. Noticing my reluctance, he motioned "come on" again while his plane began moving forward increasing its speed, and I now understood his meaning—takeoff with him.

Two seconds had elapsed and he was fast moving away from me. I had to push full throttle immediately before I lost sight of him in front of the huge radial engine. By then, he was ahead of me and fast moving out of my sight, hidden by my engine. Three hundred feet down the runway the crosswind had drifted my plane directly behind him completely obliterating his plane from my view.

When I first lost sight of him I decreased my power for a fraction of a second before realizing that I was losing precious time and runway, then I went full throttle again. Not knowing how close my prop was to his tail, I was faced with another immediate decision: to shut down the power and abort or to give my full throttle a boost of water injection. That would give another 300 horses of power and take a chance of chewing his tail off. To make matters worse, two other planes, following us in formation, were moving down the runway behind us.

When water injection was applied, the engine hesitated slightly before the extra horses took over, and was possible to kill the engine. For that reason water was not used on takeoff. With the load we were carrying it took all the runway we had, and I was fast running out of precious runway. So whether I aborted or not I ran a risk of ending up on the end of the strip rolled up in a ball of aluminum and steel.

A life—or—death decision was made in a fraction of a second and I popped the water switch forward and would have prayed if I had had time. The engine hesitated but took hold. What seemed like hours later, I was five feet over the end of the runway, airborne, struggling to stay that way.

When I rendezvoused on the leader's wing at 3,000 feet he had no idea we had just passed a crisis in our lives. After settling down, I thanked God for answering the prayer I never had a chance to make.

Sully wasn't on this mission so he and another pilot were sitting near the end of the runway watching the show. He later told me that they had told each other I wouldn't make it.

Now in Germany at 10,000 feet in battle formation, and using flak evasion, our target airdrome at Werl was spotted. Quite a bit of activity was going on down there. It looked as if our appearance caught them by surprise and they were trying to get as many of their airplanes off the ground as quickly as possible, so they wouldn't be sitting ducks on the ramp for us to destroy.

Although we still had our belly tank and bombs, the group leader called out on the radio, "This is Granite Red Leader. I'm taking my wingman to see what's going on down there."

Flying, like everything else in the service, was done by the numbers, and a ground attack was made in a particular order. If external tanks were used, they were jettisoned before the attack was begun to minimize a fuel explosion should the plane be hit, and allow more maneuverability. After releasing the external fuel tanks, the first run would be to drop the bombs, after which the plane became even more maneuverable without that extra weight. Then after the bombs were dropped, the rockets were usually released before the wing guns were used on subsequent passes. We still had our belly tank, bombs and rockets when the two of us peeled off to the right.

One German HE-111 twin-engine light bomber had just left the ground on takeoff and another was rolling down the runway following him. The first one, still climbing, had not reached cruising speed, so my leader veered left after him. I pulled right to line up with some other HE-111s still parked on the runway ready for takeoff to strafe them.

Before reaching the field I saw out of the corner of my eye, my leader's target streaming gasoline. It broke into three snap rolls and hit the ground in a burst of flame. He hit his target! I could confirm that one for him. About two seconds later I saw a second burst of fire, another plane exploding in mid-air. I was already in my strafing run and busy getting lined up with the planes on the ground and dodging ground fire. I didn't fully comprehend what had happened until reflecting on it a moment or two, but I suspected things went badly for my leader.

I had, by now, begun the strafing run toward the planes on the runway with almost 2,000 pounds of extra weight. The dive would be fast, and the climb would be tediously slow with the added weight, but I was committed.

With ground fire coming from all directions, I strafed several planes on the ground and pulled up into a climb. Tracers from the ground surrounded the plane as I struggled to get out of range. I was amazed that none hit me, and wondered when one would. Climbing with the extra weight of two 500-lb bombs and the sloshing gasoline under me, the Jug seemed to be suspended in space, a sitting duck for the ground fire, but miraculously none hit me.

It seemed to take forever getting to 6,000 feet just below a cloud layer, when I finally jettisoned the external fuel tank. I sighed a great relief, still wondering why I wasn't hit by the intensive ack – ack.

Marshaling yards where supply trains converge were high priority targets, often well defended by heavy flak. Their destruction impeded the delivery of supplies, ammunition and troops to the front. (U.S.A.F.)

I realized now that my leader was lost. Thunderbolts filled the air swarming like angry bees, and I couldn't distinguish my squadron from any other. I still had armament and had to put it to use, so I attached myself to the nearest group of Jugs bombing a nearby marshaling yard. We dropped our bombs then made passes with our rockets and machine guns. Finally, low on ammo, I headed back home alone, as none of the other P – 47s were going my way. The buddy system had to be violated this time.

The special orders awarding me the Distinguished Flying Cross for this mission said something about "unusual courage" and "determination." I was determined, alright, but unusual courage had nothing to do with it.

Two rivers, the Rhine and Meuse, both generally running north and south, were used for landmarks on the return trips from our missions. The Rhine River was still in enemy territory and very well protected by a heavy concentration of anti – aircraft guns. The Meuse River in Belgium was on the friendly side of the line. Once the Meuse was reached, our field at St. Trond was almost in sight.

Heading west and still using flak evasion, I saw a lone P-38 traveling east into Germany. I wondered what a lone plane was doing crossing from friendly to enemy territory, but we wobbled our wings in salute and I felt safe again. Soon I spotted a river and almost slumped in the cockpit with relief. I discontinued the flak evasion maneuvers and headed for home, " fat, dumb and happy."

Enemy radar could track a flight path and altitude of a plane if it flew in a predictable path for a period of time. They were able to judge with reasonable accuracy where the plane would be by the time their anti-aircraft projectile reached its target. Direct hits on fighter planes were infrequent, but near misses could be as deadly, if the missile exploded near enough to the plane. A rule of thumb was that it took the projectile about one second for each 1,000 feet of altitude it traveled. To evade flak, we flew straight and level for no more than one second for each 1,000 feet of altitude above the ground, then turned to a different direction.

One of the prime rules of flying was to keep one's head moving "on a swivel" from left to right and from up to down continuously. It was to prevent mid-air collisions in heavy traffic and to know where he was at all times. Be aware of what is happening all around. Always be alert. Prevent surprises. Keep the head on a swivel at all times. My head kept moving on a swivel looking all around as a matter of training.

Suddenly while looking behind me I saw three puffs of black smoke following my flight path, bursting at about one second intervals. Knowing that their ack-ack was shot in bursts of four in a straight line, I immediately pulled my plane hard to the right, escaping the fourth burst that exploded precisely where my plane would have been in straight flight. It immediately became clear that I was still over enemy territory, having mistaken the Rhine River for the Meuse.

Everything happened so fast that I could hardly believe it happened. Even now, I must think in slow motion to get it all in. It was obvious that my straight and level flying had given them plenty of time to track me with their radar.

Everything taught to pilots was aimed toward safety, and we had a solid year of intensive training before getting our wings. After that, safety training was constant. There was no excuse for my assumption that I was in friendly territory. The two rivers are not at all alike. I had flown the route numerous times, and to have let my guard down then was unforgivable.

After the interrogation I went to the group leader's crew chief to break the news of his pilot's loss. After visiting with the crew chief and reviewing the events of the day, I wondered if the leader had known this would be his last mission. He seemed preoccupied when he motioned me to takeoff in formation with him in the strong crosswind. The external fuel tank was not jettisoned before our first run at the target.

The crew chief told me that his pilot's ritual when climbing into the cockpit was to hand his hat to the chief and say, "Take care of this for me 'til I get back." That day he handed his cap to the chief and said, "Here, I won't be needing this anymore."

Saturday 9 December 1944

It was Saturday night and time for our weekly party and dance at the officers' mess. The music was furnished by the "Nix Compris," a talented group of misplaced musicians trying to win the war with their clarinets and drums. Nurses stationed at the military hospital in Liege were brought over to join the festivities.

The Nix Compris dance band helped relieve the tension of a long week's flying by playing for the Saturday night dance. (Leap Off)

Sully, Frank, Ed and I had already bought our two bottles of champagne each and were settled for the evening. Most of the nurses were spoken for by previous arrangement with other guys who had dated them before. The rest of them were caught by the more aggressive men as they got off the truck, so we were left with each other's company.

Drinking was never my strong point, but I enjoyed a drink now and then. Two bottles of champagne were more than enough for the evening with a huge headache the next morning for good measure. Drinking made me friendly, and people I never saw before became my close buddies. Ed was always the quiet, serious one, but half a bottle would open him up. Sully never changed. He became more gregarious after drinking but was always friendly and easy to laugh.

Frank was the perfect model of an alcohol—induced change of personality. Sober, he was good-natured and amiable, a follower among us, but when he had a few drinks, he became aggressive, sometimes to the point of downright domination. Such was the mood of the evening.

As the evening progressed and our characters changed, someone suggested food. The kitchen was closed for the evening and the food was stored in a walk—in refrigerator in the room next to the makeshift dance floor. Leaving the party, we found the walk—in unlocked, and proceeded to gorge ourselves with left over chicken. There was no need to keep quiet as the racket of the band playing, dancing and noises from the dance floor covered our activities. The guys around the crap table begged for their point to come up.

Sitting around eating and in the course of a discussion about holding one's liquor, Frank called Sully a soda—popper, to which Sully took offense. One thing led to another, and after a few words, Sully and Frank were discussing the merits of a fight. They agreed that the way to settle the argument was to have a fight right there in the kitchen, so Sully offered to let Frank throw the first punch gratis to officially begin the contest. Frank, with his legs wide apart for balance, pointing his finger at his own protruding chin, gave Sully the same offer. Before Frank could finish the offer, Sully drew back and clipped him solidly on the chin.

Sully had played football in high school and college, and with continued physical training in the service, was a solid mass of muscle, and didn't know his own strength. He thought he had merely tapped Frank, but he went down with the only blow of the fight, breaking his jaw.

Sully, not knowing the extent of Frank's injury, went over to help him up and finish the evening, the argument already forgotten. He soon realized that Frank needed medical attention, not another drink. We took him to the flight surgeon, who diagnosed the injury as a broken jaw and sent him to the hospital for repairs.

From the very first word of the argument through the time Frank went into the hospital and thereafter, there was never any thought of unfairness, revenge or hard feelings from either of them. The experience cemented relationships as an event to be laughed about later.

Monday 11 December 1944

The first mission of the day was to drop leaflets, led by the operations officer with only four planes. Special bombs were loaded with leaflets advising the Germans how the war was going and giving them instructions on how to surrender without bloodshed. We were about to overrun their positions and wanted to make their surrender as easy as possible.

Neither leaflet nor escort missions happened very often as the P–47 was best suited for dive bombing and support of the army, but we did as we were told, even deliver papers.

Leaflet missions were considered somewhat easier as there was usually no fighting involved. The planes were always loaded with ammunition, and targets of opportunity were always fair game. I had never flown a leaflet mission before and looked forward to dropping harmless bombs for a change, since nobody on the ground would be hurt by it. This was to be my fun mission and I looked forward to it. The target area was in the path of our ground forces and the leaflets were to be delivered to soften the Germans' stance, and help them make the decision to surrender.

Arriving over the target, we peeled off in a straight line of four planes, dropped the bombs and began our climb back to rendezvous. The Germans' anti–aircraft guns didn't seem to have tracked us very accurately as the black puffs were bursting a safe distance away. So it was a great shock to me when suddenly my plane seemed to explode with a deafening explosion. I was hit by flak!

"OH MY GOD!" My immediate reaction was to yell at the top of my voice. I thought I yelled with such force that the strapped–on oxygen mask must have been blown away from my face an inch or so before snapping back in place. The explosion was accompanied by what sounded like a thousand fragments of flak rattling around in the cockpit for a long time. The brain works faster than one would imagine under those conditions, and what seemed a long time was actually only a fraction of a second. When the noise stopped, only the sound of the engine could be heard, which seemed muffled compared to the explosion I had just heard.

I made an inspection of the damage suffered by the plane. The first thing I noticed was a dollar–size hole in the cockpit to the left of the throttle quadrant. I tried to call the flight leader and report the hit, but couldn't get an answer.

We had now rendezvoused at 4,000 feet and I heard the leader ordering a strafing run on a train he had spotted beneath us. It was then that I realized he had not heard an earlier call. All this time my concern was to discover if there was any other damage to the plane. For all I knew the wings could have been hanging by the control cables and the tail half gone. Would it survive a dive attack?

Not knowing the extent of the damage, I decided to stay aloft and wait for the others to finish their strafing. While circling for the dive on the train, I noticed that the wire on the throttle handle had been cut by the flak. That was the radio transmission wire, and prevented radio transmission, but the receiver was operating.

While inspecting for more damage to the plane, I noticed a hole in the left arm of my flight jacket and another hole in the right thigh of my jump suit. On closer inspection I discovered a piece of flak imbedded in the thick parachute harness that crossed over the center of my chest. I had been hit in two places and scared in another, but didn't realize it until seeing it. Now the arm and leg had begun to sting a little. Had the flak missed the parachute harness by an inch it would have hit me in the chest.

Having heard stories about soldiers getting their legs blown off, unaware they were hit, with some concern I tried to find out the extent of the injuries. I was still using both arms and legs, so I knew they had not been blown off. But I didn't know how serious the injuries were. They were not hurting much, so that problem could wait.

The only noticeable damage to the plane was a dollar–size hole; what could not be seen and not being able to communicate was bothering me. The Jug had kept running and the wings had not fallen off, so when the other planes came back up after destroying the train, all I could do was to get into formation and go back home.

While flying back, one of my random thoughts was that we were doing the Germans a service on this trip with no intention of hurting anyone, and they were shooting to kill. It didn't seem fair, somehow.

TRANSLATION

Frontpoſt

> "The strong need not fear the truth"
> Ernst Moritz Arndt

March No 2   Number 30 – 12 AU

NEWS FOR GERMAN SOLDIERS, PUBLISHED BY THE AMERICAN FORCES IN WESTERN EUROPE

Collapse on the Rhine

Americans in Cologne

PARIS. — The German front West of the Rhine has collapsed. From Cologne to Xanthen the Allies stand on the Rhine. Germans hold only scattered bridgeheads. To the south the Third U. S. Army pressed on from Trier.

Muenchen-Gladbach, Krefeld Taken

After a rapid advance through the Westwall the American Ninth Army has taken M u e n - c h e n - G l a d b a c h and K r e f e l d and has joined the First Canadian Army troops advancing from Cleve and Goch. In the pocket formed by this juncture the German First Parachute Army as well as the German Fifteenth Army were wiped out. More than 60,000 Germans gave up. The total of German losses amounts to more than 100,000.

Bridges Blown Up

The First US Army which has crossed the Erft Canal surged from the West and Southwest toward Cologne. Armored units and Infantry have penetrated in two places the interior of Cologne itself. Zuelpich, Euskirchen and Frechen were taken. All Rhine bridges North of Cologne, except the bridge near Wesel, were either blown up by the Germans themselves or destroyed by the Allied Forces.

Trier Taken

Farther South the Third US Army took Trier and advanced further. The Seventh Army occupied Forbach and stands 3¼ km West of Saarbruecken on its advance into the interior of the Saar area.

Ruhr Under Fire

In Cologne, the third largest city in Germany, are important factories producing cables, tanks, aircraft, U-boat motors, railroad car and locomotive industries. The four Rhine harbors of Cologne were of the greatest importance during the fuel shortage as well as the harbor of Duisburg–Ruhrort, all of which have now been put out of use. The biggest furnaces of the Ruhr are now within reach of Allied artillery.

Russians in Stargard

MOSCOW. — On its rapid advance through Pomerania the forces of the Army Groups of Rokossowsky and Zhukov have reached the Baltic Sea near Kolberg and Koeslin. The Germans in the area of Danzig are encircled.

Red Army Advancing on Stettin

Advancing Eastward the Russians have taken Stargard and Neugard and threaten Stettin. East of the Oder River the Russians rule all Germany from the Baltic St. to Moravia. Encircled German units are still in the area of Libau, Koenigsberg and Danzig.

Koenigsberg Cut Off

In spite of desperate attempts to break out of the pocket of Koenigsberg the circle around the town is drawn tighter. The pocket was formed at Danzig after the Russians cut the main railroad route between Danzig and Stettin and had broken though to the Baltic Sea near Schlawe. The fortified strong-points of Koeslin and Kolberg as well as Pyritz and Pollnow were captured.

By this advance the Russian bulge, furthest West near Frankfurt on Oder was straightened out. The Soviets right flank is developing in the direction of Stettin. Stettin, itself, is threatened by the fall of Stargard.

Inside Breslau

Inside the encircled town of Breslau the Russians made further advances. More than half the town already is in Russian hands.

One thousand Russian workers in Dresden upon a heavy Allied air raid overwhelmed sentries at the factory in which they worked, procured weapons and ammunition at the railroad warehouse of the town, blew up an ammunition dump as well as a bridge near Kottbus and eventually fought their way through to the Russian lines.

12. H. C. KARTE

This is the English translation of the type of leaflets delivered to German troops in bombs to inform them of the progress of the war.

Back on the ground I told my crew chief of the damage and asked him to double check it for any unnoticed damages. By this time, I had determined that my injuries were minor and could wait until after the interrogation before going to the flight surgeon.

It was during the interrogation that the others first learned I had been hit and didn't go down with them to strafe the train. To them it was just another routine mission, but to me it was one I would remember in detail.

The requirement for being awarded the Purple Heart Medal was to be injured in combat, and I qualified for that. I gave a lot of thought, though, to the fact that I was being awarded the same medal for minor injuries that some other servicemen had received posthumously.

Lucky pilots of the 404th Fighter Group returned with damage to their planes and reaffirmed their respect for the Jug. (Leap Off)

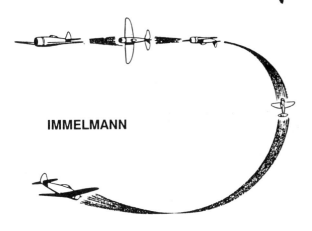

IMMELMANN

CHAPTER SIX

BATTLE OF THE BULGE

Sunday 17 December 1944

> *"There was a virtual blackout on news from the 'Bulge.' Press reports were at least 48 hours behind the events; even official reports on the situation lagged from 24 to 36 hours. The Germans were reported exploiting their penetrations in the Monschau, Malmedy–Stavelot and St. Vith sectors, cutting off the 106th Division, and surrounding the 101st Airborne at Bastogne."*
>
> *(Leap Off, 404th FG History)*

The German offensive, the Battle of the Ardennes, later called the Battle of the Bulge, actually started 16 December, but the limited news trickled down to us slowly and was just starting to reach us. It wasn't clear just what was happening, but we knew it was something big.

The war had been going so much in favor of the Allies since D–Day that there was no reason to believe it would change. Yet, reports indicated that German troops and vehicles were sighted at Stavelot, Belgium, 25 miles inside where our lines were two days earlier.

Even in the confusion of surprise attack, it was almost unbelievable how quickly Allied commanders assessed the situation and moved thousands of men, once they had enough information to act.

Immediately, the 506th Squadron was sent to Stavelot, where "Rosalee," the 506th ground control liaison pilot, called for an aerial attack on Germans. They were coming with columns of tanks, trucks, mounted guns and horsedrawn vehicles. Upon the pilots' return at the interrogation, they claimed thirteen vehicles, but when this position was taken later by the Allies, forty vehicles were counted.

I was not on the group's first mission of the day, which was to hit an airfield southeast of Bonn, near Euskirchen. It was reported to be the German base from which they were raiding the U.S. First Army, and an important target. I attended the interrogation when they returned.

The operations officer who led the group reported that he had ordered the three squadrons to different levels to protect each other as they approached the target. They did not reach the airfield because the Luftwaffe had anticipated their arrival and were in the air ready for them. An air battle ensued between the P–47s and over 50 Me–109s and FW–190s, filling the sky with aircraft chasing each other.

One pilot reported that there were so many planes in the air that it looked as if they would have to signal with their arms to make turns. They reported a floor of flak so thick over Euskirchen it could be walked on. German anti–aircraft guns added to the confusion by a flak barrage endangering their own aircraft as well as ours.

Early in the fight, the group leader shot down two Me–109s while the 508th Squadron leader split–S'ed into six Me–109s, coming in behind them and shooting down the trailing plane.

One pilot was on the tail of an Me–109 in a Lufberry circle, a circling maneuver, then suddenly found himself leading two Germans who were peppering him with their guns from behind. He escaped by diving at a steep angle.

Another pilot of the 508th Squadron was heard to call on his radio, "I've got three cornered over here." and a moment later, was heard to plead, "Someone help me! I've got three on my tail!" He managed to evade them by hitting the deck and staying there all the way back to A–92.

Another pilot reported that he had shot the tail off an FW–190 and that the pilot had literally sprung out of its cockpit. The P–47 pilot recalled, "He looked silly, sitting in the middle of space, looking at me with a surprised look on his face as his 'chute opened."

Claims for that mission were six enemy aircraft destroyed and seven damaged with no losses of our planes. These claims were in addition to the armed vehicles destroyed on the ground.

I was on the second mission and the intelligence officer at the briefing pointed to Euskirchen on the wall map and told us that we were to make sure the town was completely destroyed. Two 500-lb bombs and one 260-lb fragmentation bomb plus the eight rockets and eight .50 caliber guns, standard equipment on all missions were to be carried. Because of the heavy flak, the intelligence officer ordered bombs to be dropped from no lower than 2,000 feet. From that altitude, any direct hit on a small target would be almost an accident.

The German "last ditch" offensive had begun in earnest and Euskirchen was a big part of it, although at our level as pilots, we didn't know the immensity of the attack. After we returned from the mission it was explained that the Germans had moved everything they could muster, even from the Russian front, into this area for their offensive.

It was apparent that even if their push succeeded in driving farther into Belgium, it would be almost impossible for them to sustain an advance beyond their supply lines. We were cutting rail lines and daily strafing roads. Nevertheless, they were fanatical in their belief that they could take a large part of the territory they once held. Convinced they were defending their homeland gave them a great incentive to fight. And fight, they did.

Euskirchen was about 75 miles from our base and we could see black clouds of smoke and red flames from several miles away before we got there. That confirmed the intelligence officer's briefing a few minutes earlier. By the time we were readying our bomb run, the flak was so thick that the IO's order came back to me loud and clear, "Don't go below 2,000 feet to drop your bombs." (Ground school had taught us that we could fly through the harmless puffs of black smoke from flak bursts since the fragments of steel had already dispersed, but a psychological block discouraged the practice. What if there were still some fragments just waiting for my plane to plow into it?)

When we got over the target, Thunderbolts from other groups in addition to the 404th, were dropping their bombs from every altitude, and then continuing to dive to the deck to strafe.

Our squadron separated into flights of four planes to operate independently and our flight began its bombing dive from about 8,000 feet. Heading below, we dropped our bombs at 2,000 feet and continued on through the flak and fire to strafe on the deck. The smoke was so thick that I couldn't see where my bombs fell but the flight leader confirmed that the bombs resulted in a rail cut. There was a little flak damage but no losses on this mission, but two men and two planes from the 508th were lost on an earlier one. With all the activity going on at Euskirchen, I believe it was destroyed as it was ordered.

Procedure upon the return from a mission was that pilots went to the ready room for an interrogation by the squadron intelligence officer, S-2, to determine the damage to the target. All incidents and any unusual activity were reported. The pilots put in their claims of targets destroyed or damaged, and from this information, the S-2 made his report.

Then the mission leader held a critique on the complete mission, from taxiing out until the landing of the last plane. He pin-pointed any faults observed in takeoff, join-up, flight formation to the target, action over the target, flight formation on the return, peel-off and landing. In other words, we were graded on our performance.

After landing, planes were checked over by the crew chiefs, armorers and radiomen, and all battle-damage and mechanical problems were reported. Operations was then notified of any changes in any aircraft's status so the schedule for the next mission could be set up.

The confirmed score for the 404th FG was thirty-four German aircraft destroyed or damaged, two pilots and two P-47s lost. There was also uncounted damage on the ground. More often than not, the claims figures were smaller than the actual losses, as they had to be confirmed by either gun cameras or other pilots. Several others limped back home with heavy damage to their planes, giving a lot of the credit to the Thunderbolt, the Jug.

In the evening, a German Me-262, the only operational jet fighter in the war, was observed at 6,000 feet over our field. We learned later that this was probably an observation flight to prepare the Jerries for an attack on our field.

Monday 18 December 1944

Bad weather grounded us for the next few days. Because of the lack of aerial support during this period, the Germans were able to make advances into our territory, and our army had to give up ground.

Tuesday 19 December 1944

Enemy–damaged bombers, both American and British Royal Air Force, were regular visitors to our field, as we were one of the nearest on our side of the bomb line and on the airway to Germany. When a plane came in, wounded would be taken off and treated and damage to the aircraft repaired enough to ferry it back to its base or scrapped.

A B–17 Flying Fortress came towards our field firing flares, signalling wounded aboard, and needed to land at once. We could tell that the pilot was having a hard time controlling the plane as part of a wing was gone and one engine had its prop blown off. The field was readied for his emergency landing and emergency vehicles rushed toward the end of the runway. As it approached, the pilot seemed to be fighting the controls to keep it on course for a landing. Despite having ineffective controls and a prop lost, he made a beautiful landing. His brakes were obviously gone, and he used the full length of the runway in his landing roll.

"Big Friend" lands at St. Trond with one more man than when it took off. The body of a man from another plane was thrown through the B–17 in mid–air. (Leap Off)

A battle–damaged B–24 Liberator that had landed several days earlier, was parked near the end of the runway, waiting to be moved. The B–17 pilot, apparently seeing the other plane in his path, managed to groundloop his plane, but still crashed into the B‑24, bursting both planes in flames. There were no survivors.

Friday 22 December 1944

> *"An unusual type of air activity had held the attention of the group for some time. It started about noon a couple of months ago when an odd and unfamiliar rocket was heard for the first time, a sort of loud, grumbling noise, which sounded like a four‑motored bomber with engine trouble. It was our first experience with the German jet‑propelled 'V‑1 Buzz Bomb.' Late that night two more came over, thundering and vibrating as if they were going to take the tops of the buildings off."*
>
> *(Leap Off, 404th FG History)*

The sound of a buzz bomb cannot be described, it must be heard to know what it's like. It was a deep‑throated pulsating roar heard from many miles away, and seemed as loud from five or more miles away as it did from one. By the time it was close as two or three miles, it sounded as if it was overhead. The amount of measured fuel in this rocket‑propelled missile determined its range. When the fuel was exhausted, the buzz bomb dropped straight down.

It was impossible to tell when the fuel would burn out. (The Germans hoped it would fall on our field) They were also filled with different amounts of fuel to drop on other targets.

Each man had his own way to deal with the problem. Some just stood or sat still holding their breath waiting for it to drop. Others took cover. The 508th parachute rigger had dug a foxhole just outside his parachute shack and he could be found lying in his foxhole from the time he first heard the buzz bomb until it exploded. Others hoped and prayed it would not land where they were.

This conversation was overheard during a buzz bomb attack:

"Here comes another one."

"No, that's an airplane."

"Oh yeah? I never heard an airplane that sounded...oh, oh, it stopped."

"Well, there it went off. I'll bet that was five miles away."

"Five miles, hell! That wasn't an inch over two miles. Why, the one just before this, sounded....oh, oh! Here comes another one!"

We had been grounded by bad weather since the 19th and had received enough skimpy news to realize the seriousness of the situation near Stavelot. Group Commander Colonel Moon called a meeting to announce that XXIX TAC, the next level of command above group, anticipated a 1,500 paratrooper attack on A-92 and another field at any time.

Tension was not eased when Colonel Moon said of the possible invasion, "Personally, I'd like to see about a thousand Germans try to come down on our field. I know we're not trained combat troops but we'll make it interesting for them if they try it. Of course, some men will be killed. We must expect that." He then briefed the group on Plans A and B to evacuate in the event of such an attack.

Some of the apprehension was relieved knowing that 700 infantry troops were quartered east of our field and British tank units had moved in a couple of miles down the road.

Information of the Germans' strength was supported when one of our ground crew members who had been serving as a member of an air support team with the 2nd Armored Tanks reported that a German patrol in captured American uniforms using American jeeps and tanks had been seen south of St. Vith. We were now on alert to expect anything from the Jerries.

Saturday 23 December 1944

Mail was being forwarded to us from our previous posts and we were getting letters in bunches. Mail might take from five days to three months to reach us, stacking up in ports along the way. They were delivered when our location was known. Letters from home written two days to three months apart had to be read in chronological order to make any sense.

We didn't care how old the letters were, nor when they were written, just as long as they got to us. Our biggest complaint about the folks back home was that they didn't write often enough. Little did we know that they had been writing, but we were not getting all our mail. Some was lost at sea in ships being sunk on their way with mail and other supplies. Some was stolen, especially the packages, for the valuables they had in them. Other mail was stacked up someplace, delayed and delivered when it could be.

Those letters delivered were relished and read over and over again, injecting another bit of home into our souls to keep us going for another day.

Bill had been located at Nadzab in New Guinea, where the fighting had already been and was not likely to return; and Cecil had now been located behind the lines in Italy, so we didn't have to worry about them being in too much danger.

V-1 rockets, buzz bombs, were filled with a measured amount of jet
fuel to fly to a predetermined target. When the fuel was exhausted
it fell straight down and exploded on impact. These remarkable
pictures caught the jet-powered buzz bomb flying low just before its
fuel was exhausted, and in the second picture, after it had run out
of fuel as it was falling down before impact. (Leap Off)

The family was still passing hints in the letters. I knew Cecil was in Europe, and pretty sure in Italy, but to win the game, I had to find his exact spot there. A letter from home told me that he was in a "fog" about where he was, but didn't offer any other information. Looking at the map, it was obvious that he was stationed near Foggia. He had told us that he was a supply sergeant, so we were relieved to believe he would be safe from fighting.

Jimmie and I were in Europe where the fighting was moving fast, so it would be hard to keep up with us. I knew where I was, and Jim, I suppose, knew where he was, but nobody else in the family knew. I was the closest to him and everytime I heard from him he had moved someplace else. So I knew that locating him would have to wait until he settled down in one place for awhile.

Jimmie was with the Military Police and helped guard German prisoners, and direct truck convoys on their way to the front, often ahead of our advancing armies. With each letter from him I would almost pinpoint him, but the next letter would send me back to the maps. Settling down to a permanent base of operations was not in the books for Jim for awhile.

I thought I could ask questions of those in higher positions in headquarters to find him, but even headquarters couldn't help. I would just have to wait. I knew the time would come when Jimmie would be found, and we would have our own family reunion.

Far from home, memories of family were constantly resurfacing, and with Christmas approaching, these thoughts came more often.

Mama, who immigrated to the United States from Lebanon in 1900, was determined to learn to read and write English for her sons in the service. She came to America knowing how to speak, read and write only Arabic, learning to speak English by necessity. She had met and married Papa in the United States, bore him nine children (one died in infancy) and was a homemaker who believed she needed no other formal education.

An Arabic newspaper was one of her links to the world. For other links, she listened to the radio. Her children and husband discussed current events with her. Her social life centered around the Methodist Church, her friends and neighbors, so there had been no need to learn more. After all, her husband knew everything.

That was until she sent four sons to the service who constantly complained in their letters that they did not get enough mail from home. At first, she depended on Papa and the three girls to write her messages. She felt that was not personal enough, so, after forty–two years in America, she went to school to learn to read and write English for her boys in the service.

Mama was a person of determination and confidence and knew she could do anything anyone else could do, barring physical limitation. She would look at someone else's handiwork, be it sewing, cooking or other creation, and copy it, sometimes as well as the original, or better, adding her own personality to it. It would be no different with her studies. Her first letters to us were grammatically correct, obviously coached by a teacher or one of her daughters. Others were copies, in her own handwriting, of The Psalms.

Then there were the ones written straight from the heart, written on lined paper from a small note pad. Sentence structure was ignored and spelling was phonetically written in her unique broken English. The message came from her soul. Those letters revealed her innermost thoughts. It was Mama actually talking to us, and we heard every inflection in her broken English. (We teased her by saying she had been in America longer than we had, and we could speak better English than she could) When I wanted to feel back home – really back home – I would lie on my bunk and re–read her letters over and over, savoring each word.

Mama's overwhelming love for her family was shown by the determination and purpose for which she learned English. She had no reason before, but now, she couldn't hide the pain of loss and the love for her family any longer, and was determined to do something about it.

Letters sent to the men in the service were all–important, but none was more cherished than those written by Mama, solely out of love.

Among the letters was another from Papa, bringing back memories of personal events between only Papa and me. With eight children, it would seem that a parent's love would necessarily be collective for the family as a unit. Not so with Papa. Each of his children held a special place in his heart and each could tell of incidents with him that weren't shared by any of the others.

Papa was eighteen years old and alone when he migrated to America from Lebanon in the steerage of a steamship in 1895. After arrival he educated himself in the ways of his new world, found a wife, also from Lebanon, and established a family to share their new life together.

The obstacles in the forty–six years he had been in his adopted country were many and varied, and he dealt with them in the only way he knew how: by facing them one by one with hard work and determination until they had been eliminated or tolerably eased. He had become a successful businessman, but more importantly, a successful family man, and good American citizen.

Four of the eight children they reared to adulthood had now left for the military. They were proud of the four–starred placard placed in the front window to tell the world about their men in the service. Now Papa had a problem he couldn't solve by hard work, no matter how hard he tried. He couldn't furnish us the safety net he wanted so desperately to. Neither he nor any of us in the service had any control over where we would be tomorrow. He felt helpless having to stay home and wonder if the next correspondence he would receive would be a telegram from the War Department reading, "We regret to inform you..."

When each of us left home, Papa gave a deeper meaning to the prayer, "God be with you, son. Come back safely."

His letters to "My Dear Son Kemal" gave the progress of his victory garden, saying "the strawberries and figs are coming along nicely, and the grapes are doing very well....we'll have some wine when you come home...Jimmie's last letter said he had a new address and Cecil was doing fine....we heard from Billie in the South Pacific....Kemal, please be careful....Your Mother and your sisters give you their love and Grandma sends you a big hug....Your Dad loves you."

Newsy, to the point and, between the lines, the constant concern for my safety. He didn't intend his feelings to come through so clearly, but they were loud and clear to me. His concern for me translated into my concern for him.

Papa was a strong person but he was a "softy" when it came to his family. He showed so much regard for his family that I believed his life would be devastated by the loss of any member. Because of this belief, my thoughts after any close call were instinctively of Papa and how he would take any bad news.

It would be a lie to say I had no fear, but I was more concerned how Papa would take the loss of a son than I was for my own safety. That had a calming affect on me.

Sunday 24 December 1944 Christmas Eve

A civilian Christmas Eve with five boys, three girls and Mama and Papa had always meant fun with the family: talking, laughing, playing and waiting for midnight to roll around to open gifts. Since we had all become adults, the joy of opening gifts early Christmas morning had been moved forward six hours earlier to midnight, Christmas Eve.

This year the family was spread over five countries and three continents and was the first Christmas away from home for some of us. Each of us, wherever we were, no doubt were thinking the same thoughts and remembering past Christmases.

This Christmas Eve found me and others in the mess hall where movies were shown about three times a week, enjoying a thriller that was about over. We were still waiting to find out who dunnit when a man burst in the mess hall screaming, "Stop the Show! There are German paratroopers on the four corners of the field!"

Immediately lights went on and there was a mad scramble for the nearest exit. In the rush, Junior fell down and was almost trampled right where he fell until a couple of us came to his rescue. We were stunned and confused but knew that we must get to the barracks about 200 feet away and get our guns and organize to guard the chateau. We dashed outside calling to each other to make sure where our buddies were.

The heavy fog that had covered the ground had cleared by now. The dry air was bitterly cold and there was not a wisp of wind nor a cloud in the sky. It was about 10 p.m. and the full moon made it dusk – bright. In the rush and excitement, random thoughts ran through my mind: What a way to spend Christmas Eve. Is this really happening to me? It would be a great night for a date.

The news of the German offensive was being constantly fed to us as available. Updated maps showed that if the Germans, who were about fifty – five miles southeast of us, continued their drive in a straight line, they would cross our runways.

Having been warned to expect anything from them, including paratroopers, in their last ditch effort, it was now happening. Briefings had included Plans A and B. Plan A was an orderly retreat allowing for as many pilots as there were flyable planes to go a safe distance west to another field from which the group would operate. Under this plan all other personnel would follow in trucks and evacuate the field.

Plan B was to be used only in case of surprise and extreme emergency. As many pilots as possible would fly out taking their crew chiefs with them in the one – man cockpit by sitting on the chief's lap instead of using a parachute as a seat. Everyone who did not fly out would remain and defend the departing planes. Those left behind were on their own.

In a very few minutes the pilots of the 508th Squadron were organized into different shifts of guard duty to guard our living quarters. Soon it was surrounded so well that we were challenging each other. Guarding my corner of the building in the bright moonlight, I felt conspicuously on stage and an easy target for an unseen enemy.

From the moment we got our weapons some men became trigger-happy and were ready to shoot anything that didn't answer the challenge. Sporadic firing from .45 automatics and bursts from machine guns were heard from every direction around us. Most of the shots came from the runway area, and we guessed that the paratroopers were attacking our aircraft.

By now, Plan B was out of the question. There was no Plan C.

The cold air was so uncomfortable that we rotated our guard shifts often to warm our seats in front of the huge fireplace before taking our posts again. After awhile our fears of the paratroopers gave way to the fear that we would have to stand outside in the cold all night waiting to be attacked. The suspense was getting the best of us. It might have been better, we thought, if at least one paratrooper would surface so we would have a reason to stay on guard.

During a break in guard duty, Sully and I and three others were resting on the eight-foot couch in front of the fireplace. One of our pilots had found his courage in a bottle of booze and was feeling no pain. In his condition, he was confident that he could hold off the attacking paratroopers single-handedly. Wisely, he was not assigned a guard post as we were. Instead he would go outside screaming for the dirty enemy to come out and fight like real soldiers. With his .45 automatic pistol waving in the air, he would show them. From time to time, he would come into the chateau threatening his own friends with his cocked gun. We did our best to calm him down.

He was on the couch when Sully and I came in from the cold to rest and get warm. Reading from left to right on the couch were Bob, Sully, me, our drunken companion and Denzil. This time I was the one to try to get him to calm down, but he took drunken offense at my suggestion and stood up, pulling his gun from its holster.

"I'll show you how to kill a man," he announced. He then drew back his gun to hit me on the head with the side of the gun. With one motion, the others stood up and Sully reached in front of me and grabbed his arm while Denzil, on the drunk's left, grabbed his other arm and held him off. He calmed down immediately and within a short while was asleep on the couch.

After getting warm I was back on guard duty, standing in some bushes and wishing I was in bed, when the loud speaker sounded the "all clear." What seemed like ten hours was actually less than two. Back inside we were told what had really happened.

Appearing from the east like The Star of Bethlehem on that Christmas Eve, a crippled British Lancaster heavy bomber was returning from a night raid over Germany. It intended to land at our field, which was often used as a safe haven for battle–damaged aircraft. They were not able to get far enough to land, and had to bail out about four kilometers from the field.

Like the parlor game of "Gossip," where a message is whispered from one ear to the next until the final version has no semblance to the original message, "parachutes four kilometers from the field" became "paratroopers on the four corners of the field."

The men broke up soon after the all–clear sounded. Some went back to the sack and others played cards or wrote letters home. Perhaps most of them were thinking about their previous Christmases at home as I was.

Unwinding after this experience was made a little harder knowing it was Christmas Eve. It was 11:45 and I was bushed, but I waited until Midnight to greet Christmas before hitting the sack to lie on my back to fix my eyes on a darkened invisible ceiling.

On the ceiling, it seemed, was a brightly lighted Christmas tree in the living room in Oklahoma City with every vivid detail as I remembered it. Papa was sitting in his armchair enjoying seeing his children having a good time, and Mama flitted from the living room to the kitchen and back to check on the turkey. Jimmie was getting irritated trying to organize this group of rowdies.

Edna Mae and Nell were putting last minute gifts around the tree, directed by Bedelia, telling them to put the pretty green package in the front where it would show better. Ralph was adjusting his fancy camera and fussing with his new light meter. Cecil looked at the names on the packages to make sure he was getting his share.

Bill was strutting around eating a stick of celery and planning the traditional Monopoly game the boys would play into the wee hours of the night after the gift–giving was over. I was demanding that it was my turn to pass out the gifts this year.

Like all Christmases before, in my imagination, I was home with the family again, repeating our traditional Christmas rituals. I could smell the fragrance of the decorated tree mixed with the smells from the kitchen; feel the warmth of the ornate stove in the fireplace. I could hear the babble of excited voices making conversation with one group while trying to listen to another conversation, not wanting to miss any part of this reunion.

Lying on a bunk in Belgium thousands of miles away, I really didn't miss being home for Christmas after all.

Wednesday 27 December 1944

Few missions had been flown since the 18th due to bad weather. Today it was hazy on the ground but clear above 400 feet here and over the target. The second mission took off and headed toward St. Vith to support the army holed up there. When we got there, the ground controller radioed that there were tanks giving them trouble. The squadron separated into two–plane elements, and Don and I were to strafe some tanks hidden under some trees.

The haze had dissipated and the afternoon sun cast heavy shadows, and German vehicles hidden in the thick trees were hard to see. Some pilots could spot a bug crawling on the ground while some of us had to be guided to the smaller targets. Don and I were directed to a clump of trees to strafe some tanks hidden under them. We strafed enough to destroy anything there. Several more passes at other targets, and with fuel and ammo running low, the squadron headed home.

Gun cameras that were activated to take movies when the guns were fired, were mounted in one wing so all strafing would be recorded on film. The film was then analyzed by higher headquarters first, and what they didn't keep, was sent to the squadron, and eventually to the pilot who took the pictures. It took awhile for the film to come back to us, and when this particular piece of action was returned to me and I compared mine with Don's, we agreed that we had probably mistaken a heavy tree shadow for a tank under the trees, and after two passes, the shadow was still there. We decided not to put in a claim for a tree shadow. The mission was a success, however, as other targets were hit and we got some hearty thanks from the army.

BATTLE OF THE BULGE
16 December - 26 December 1944

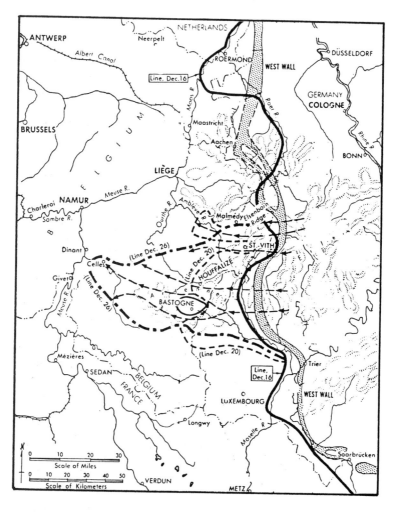

The battle line on 16 December 1944 is shown by the solid black line. Four days later, the Germans had extended their offensive push as indicated by the light dotted line. By 26 December, the bulge, extended to the Meuse River, where it was stopped.

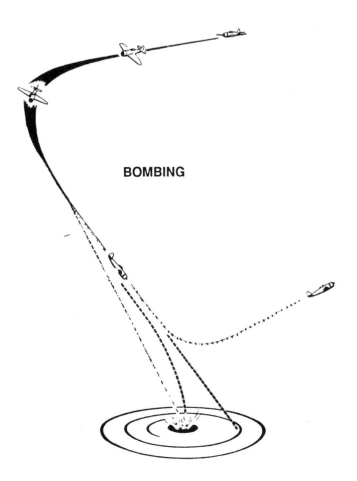

BOMBING

CHAPTER SEVEN

BEGINNING OF THE END

Monday 1 January 1945 New Years Day

It had been a rough two weeks with fewer flying days, and the Germans had given the army and tanks some pretty bad times. In spite of it, we still were spoiled into believing that nothing could stop us. It was humiliating to find the Allies on the defensive after a rapid march through France, Holland and Belgium.

The Germans, however, still hoped for some sort of victory, even though the overall picture proved they could never regain their losses and win the war. Their manpower was steadily being depleted and their industrial potential being destroyed. Because Hitler had stubbornly refused to accept his field officers' advice, he was making incoherent tactical decisions better left to his generals.

The situation was tense. We had been scared on Christmas Eve, and now additional precautions were taken to prevent surprise attacks. They included having four P-47s sitting on the end of the runway at all times on "alert," engines warm, ready for immediate takeoff at the first sign of threat. Pilots were rotated for this assignment every hour and this was Sully's day to be on alert.

They had been on alert for about an hour and were bored waiting so long without action. They were to be relieved in ten minutes, so their radios were turned off to conserve the electrical system. Runway alerts had gone on for some time now, and day after day of that duty without any scrambles made an hour-long duty pretty boring. This being New Year's Day (the morning after the Big Night), not much activity was expected.

The Germans had been very aggressive since the 16th, making a deep bulge in the bomb line, and we tried to be prepared for any attack. The group had been put on guard even before the Christmas Eve scare and was warned of other possible attacks.

I was not due for a mission that morning, and was in the ready room where we spent most of our time on the ground. There was a popping of arms fire from the runway area. More out of curiosity than alarm, those in the ready room rushed outside to see what was going on. By the time we reached the door, we could hear the roar of low-flying airplanes and the sound of machine guns. There were German FW-190s and Me-109s all over, from twenty feet off the ground to not more than 500 feet.

The first attack came down the runway strafing between the alert planes, missing all of them. Their second run crossed the runway at various angles down to the ground. By that time the field's anti-aircraft guns went into action.

One Me-109 came across the field on the deck from south to north shooting, flying straight and level. Halfway across the field it was hit and burst in a ball of flame, zooming straight up. The pilot bailed out and was captured when he landed. An FW-190 pilot was not so lucky. His plane crashed on the runway just a few yards from the alert planes. Sully jumped out of his plane, oblivious of the danger around him, to where the young German pilot's body had been thrown. Sully recalled later that while viewing this pilot's body still steaming in the cold air, he wondered if this would be the way it would end for him and who would be looking at his body.

The Luftwaffe had come in low under the capabilities of our radar, so there had been no advance warning of their attack. Even if there had been a warning in the ten minutes before the attack, the alert planes would not have responded because their radios were off at the time.

All the German planes were destroyed except two. One FW−190 pilot decided to surrender and landed without damage. The other, apparently the leader and the only experienced combat pilot on this mission, had escaped. All the pilots killed or captured were too young to have had much experience in combat, and had shown their lack of training.

In a well−kept secret, the Germans had long been planning this day which called for a Luftwaffe blitz on Allied airfields in Belgium and Holland, involving between 800 and 900 planes to be carried out simultaneously. Documents captured later showed that our field was to have been the primary target of 200 planes on New Year's Day. The planes that attacked us were to have hit another field, apparently through faulty navigation, or perhaps a last minute change of orders, but they struck ours.

It was also noted that a German Me−262 jet fighter had come over our field on the 17th of December, probably on a reconnaissance flight in preparation for the New Year's Day raid.

After the smoke had cleared, it was found that the ground fire had destroyed five German planes. One FW−190 was captured intact and another had escaped. The captured plane was later painted a bright red and sported the American identifying star and bar on its side.

All the excitement was not at the field that New Year's Day. The first mission had already taken off before the field was attacked and they missed the big show at home. But they had their own problems with heavy flak that accounted for the loss of one of my roommates.

Bill seemed out of place among the five of us. He was a loner and never joined in our rowdy capers. Our conversations were always friendly but never chummy. The other four knew about our respective families back home, and what our plans were when we would get out of this man's army, but discussions with Bill were of only present circumstances.

In retrospect, it could almost have been predicted that he would "buy the farm" someday, as he came back too often from missions with serious damage to his plane. He, in fact, was kidded about it. He had returned from one mission with a flak hole in the horizontal stabilizer and his picture was taken while standing in the hole. Almost all of his missions resulted in some damage to his plane. Now he had bailed out over enemy territory and was listed as Missing In Action, and nothing more was heard about him.

The story in the Air Force was that when a pilot's wings were issued, he was also issued an unknown number of takeoffs minus one landing, so when he took off he never knew whether or not he used his last landing on his previous flight. Bill used his last landing.

Tuesday 2 January 1945

The Jerries still had a lot of fight left in them, proved by yesterday's attack. A tug‑o'‑war was still going on for Bastogne. The weather had been bad the past couple of weeks and we flew only occasionally, but the past few days it cleared enough for us to get off the ground in force.

Robin was leading a flight when the 506th Squadron took off for Bastogne about noon. When they reached their target and Robin's flight began its run, the flak was intense, and halfway into his run he heard a WHAM! BANG! Two 88s exploded near his right wing that bounced his plane violently. A hard reflexive turn to the left didn't prevent one of the next two bursts from hitting his plane.

As he was going down, he heard his wingman call the squadron leader, "Jo‑Jo, I think we lost Robin going in on the target." Robin had recovered enough to prevent a crash but was in bad trouble. He tried to call Jo‑Jo to tell him he had not gone in, but the hit had knocked out his radio transmission.

With so many planes from other groups in the sky, he was separated from his own. A quick survey showed a hole in both sides of the canopy lined up with his head. He felt his head. No blood, so he was OK there, and by now the Jug was pouring out smoke and running rough. It was still flying but losing altitude slowly even with full throttle, and hydraulic fluid on the floor had ignited, causing a fire in the cockpit.

"God," Robin thought, "if there was ever a time to pray, it's now, but, God, I'm too busy flying this damned airplane to pray."

The fire was going pretty good now and he had to consider his next step, so he jettisoned the bubble canopy to prepare to bail out.

Down to about 2,500 feet and flying through two layers of clouds, he got intermittent light flak from the ground when there was a break in the clouds.

The airplane was burning badly, the engine missing and trailing smoke, and it would be time to get out of the plane before it blew up. His goggles were oiled over and he was soaked with hot hydraulic fluid and could hardly see. It was time to go, so he trimmed the plane, unbuckled his safety belt, stood in the seat and made a dive for the wing.

He hit the 160 MPH slipstream and it blew him back in the seat. He was desperate now, and grabbed the side of the cockpit and crawled out. His right leg got caught in a jagged hole in the fuselage he had overlooked, so he hung on for dear life. Kicking and working with his feet, his leg finally came free and he let go of the canopy rail, and the tail went by over his head as he fell.

Floating down, his burning plane made a slow turn to the left and hit the ground with the frag still on the belly. It exploded on impact, blowing the engine off and throwing it several hundred feet away. Some Jerries took potshots at him as he was coming down but they missed.

Seeing some civilians after landing on a snow-sprinkled hilltop and, with a .45 automatic in his hand, he asked in English, "Am I in Germany or Belgium?" He heard the welcome word "*Belgique*" and some gunfire, followed by three tanks lumbering near in the snow. After a few seconds that seemed forever, he noticed the British markings on the tanks. "Allies," he thought.

The Germans were close enough to shoot at him but after a few bursts from the tanks, they stopped. Then two tanks reached him, giving a shelter between them, protecting him from gunfire. Immediately a big arm came over the side of one of the tanks and grabbed the pistol, and with the other arm, jerked him into the tank.

Inside they yelled at Robin in German but their uniforms were British. We had known for sometime that the Germans had infiltrated our lines wearing captured American uniforms and driving captured U.S. vehicles so they assumed he was the enemy. Telling them he was a P-47 pilot named Grout, they were certain he was German. Grout the Kraut! They didn't know the huge P-47 carried a crew of only one. He eventually persuaded them that he was an American.

Their mission was a reconnaissance behind the lines and they were fighting their way back about two miles away. When they reached the safety of friendly territory, he was interrogated by the British and sent back to St. Trond.

When he reported to the squadron commander, Major Peterson and the Intelligence Officer cried out "Robin, you're dead! I have your MIA (Missing In Action) telegram and was on my way to send it to your mom and dad saying, 'We regret to inform you that on 2 January 1945, your son, Lt. Robert C. Grout, etc., etc., and presumed dead.'"

Robin was not the only one to have a good reason to remember the 2nd of January, 1945. Bob Williams was on a mission later in the day but had to abort because of a propeller problem. He returned to the field with two 500–lb bombs still attached to the wings and a frag under the belly. They had not been armed to explode on impact so he felt safe in landing with them attached, as he had done just a week before.

His only problem, he thought, was in landing with the extra weight of the bombs and full fuel tanks. To allow for it, he decided to land a little farther down the runway, but actually touched about halfway. He realized that the landing wasn't going to be a good one, having used half of the runway, so he pushed everything forward to go around. As he did, the prop, already acting up, ran away and revved up to 4500 RPM, about double the normal speed.

He knew then he was not going to get off the ground. Over half of the runway had already been used and the extra weight made it impossible to go around or make a successful emergency landing. Then Bob's mind began working so fast that everything else seemed to move in slow motion and almost every little detail could be recalled later.

He looked out the left side of the plane and noticed that the left wing was heading for a cletrac, a heavy piece of towing equipment, with a man sitting in the seat. The operator heard all the racket, noticed what was happening and looked straight at Bob with such a surprised look that Bob laughed in spite of his predicament. Like cartoons, the operator jumped straight up out of his seat and hit the ground running with his feet moving so fast they looked like wheels. Then the left wing hit the cletrac and the bomb dropped off.

Even then, he thought, "That's OK, because they haven't been armed, and won't go off."

Knowing that he could not go around, he started retracting the landing gear to belly in as he had done a week before, and was experienced in that procedure now. The electrically operated bubble canopy couldn't be opened because of the electric system failure.

When he tried to pull it back manually the latch kept hitting him on the head, and only partially opened.

The left wing hit the cletrac and there was a very loud noise. That was the bomb on the right wing. Bob nonchalantly looked to the right and thought, "Oh, the bomb went off because there is no wing left." but the plane was still sliding along the runway, wheels up.

Then, the left bomb dropped off, not exploding, and the right one had exploded blowing the right wing off. The only one left to worry about was the belly bomb, but Bob was more concerned that he was on fire.

When the plane stopped sliding down the runway, he unfastened his safety belt and was able to open the canopy manually. The next thing he remembered was that he had jumped off the left wing tip, a long way to the ground.

He never lost consciousness, and with all the commotion, thought he had better run out across the road.

The plane had gone off the end of the runway before it stopped. With his backpack parachute still strapped on, he ran toward the woods and into a barbed wire fence about four feet high. Stepping back about two steps and with a short run, he leaped over it with the cumbersome backpack still strapped on. A few steps inside the fence, his knee gave way and he collapsed.

An infantry division was bivouacked nearby and in a few seconds a super-human voice shouted to his companion, "Goddam, he's still living!"

Bending down, a soldier pulled out a trench knife and slit Bob's pant leg to examine his knee. He picked Bob up and carried him back into the woods a short distance. Soon an ambulance came and took him by the squadron operations on the way to the hospital.

At the operations office, Squadron Commander Garrigan opened the rear door expecting to see a corpse, and in a very reverent voice, asked, "Do you have Williams in there?"

"Yeah, there ain't nothing wrong with him!" the ambulance attendant answered.

Well, he was almost right. Besides having the end of his thumb blown off, a bunged-up knee and a scraped back, he was OK, and was kept in the hospital only one day.

Bob thought it was bad enough getting his airplane blown up while he was in it, but because he had aborted the mission before going across the bomb line, he did not get the Purple Heart.

Sunday 21 January 1945

With the stubborn resistance of the Allied troops in the Bulge, Germans were beginning a retreat in apparent panic. Their usual movement of troops and supplies had been at night when fighter–bombers could not see them, but now, their daylight withdrawal clogged the roads. Miles of vehicles, bumper–to–bumper, and troops moving eastward were easy targets, and relays of Thunderbolts shuttled back and forth, allowing our ground forces to move forward.

There was no problem finding targets since the weather had cleared enough for us to go out. The whole group took off and when we reached the area northeast of Duren, the group broke up into separate squadrons, then into flights. Joe's flight, with me flying as his element leader, spied a 25–car train chugging along as fast as it could toward their front lines, hoping to outrun the P–47s they knew were overhead.

Our first pass knocked out the engine, then on subsequent passes, we strafed the cars. A couple of cars exploded, throwing debris up to several thousand feet and black smoke to thousands of feet more. Finding other targets, we didn't stop until we were called to rendezvous and return to the base where I was already scheduled for another mission.

The Germans were put to rout and we furnished the momentum to continue it. Shuttle missions continued through the next two days before we were grounded by heavy snowfall. It had been a busy three days for me, Sunday, Monday and Tuesday, but advantage had to be taken when the weather permitted. In those three days, the group dropped almost 50 tons of bombs, fired over 60,000 rounds of ammo and destroyed almost 1,500 military transports and rail cars. It was not every day we could do this good.

Tuesday 23 January 1945

A second lieutenant is the lowest man on the totem pole as an officer, and we looked forward to getting out of this category as quickly as possible. We were willing to serve our time in grade but would be ready to get that first promotion as an officer.

Eight of the nine men who volunteered together back at Minter Field had been promoted to first lieutenant a week before. Not me. I had been doing the same thing they had, and deserved the same rewards. The Air Force does everything in bunches, by the numbers and in alphabetical order, so my number should have been in the same basket as the others. Clearly it was not.

Conway and Yocum and all other alphabets between in our clique – except me – had been granted the silver bars of a first lieutenant. The commanding officer assured me that my name was submitted at the same time and would be here shortly. Don't worry, he said, so I didn't. I wondered why, though.

About three days after their promotions, my flight leader told me that an order had come through for the promotion. It had not been posted on the board but I was so eager to be equal to my buddies that I pinned on the silver bars I had already acquired and was saving for this occasion.

That evening I was congratulated as they had been earlier. All that time I had the uneasy feeling that maybe, just maybe, the order really didn't come through. After all, I had not been given a copy confirming it. I had not seen it. The more I thought about it, the uneasier I became, and before the evening was over, my cherished silver bar was replaced with the gold one I had worn for so long.

The next day, there was still no order. Nor the next and the next. Sometimes rewards come a little slowly, and finally, it came through. That time, I made certain I got a copy of it before putting on my silver bars.

Thursday 25 January 1945

There are rules of war between enemies that are usually adhered to pretty closely, like the treatment of prisoners of war. Another was that if military personnel were caught in civilian clothes they were assumed to be spies and could be shot. I do not know what the rule is if one side is caught with his enemy's uniforms on, but that was done during the Battle of The Bulge. I assume that another rule of war was that both sides could play tricks to fool the enemy if they can get away with it.

The Germans had a strong radio signal that covered a large part of Europe and we listened to it because it had good music. A regular feature on their station was a monologue in English by "Lord Haw Haw," a British voice that interrupted the music periodically for a commentary.

After one of the Allies' big missions, Lord Haw Haw would announce in a friendly voice, the results of the mission, naming some of the Allied men who were lost, and whether they were killed or taken prisoner. He sometimes mentioned the prison they were taken to. He often named the unit that participated, where their home base was, the home town of the prisoners, and other information that was thought to be confidential.

He stressed our losses and minimized the damage we had inflicted, and the information was available to him before some of us knew about it. Wherever he got the information, some of it was uncannily true. We believed that Lord Haw Haw had a roster of every fighting unit in Europe, with our names, ranks and serial numbers.

The Allies had the last laugh on Lord Haw Haw, however, as he was subsequently captured and hung.

Occasionally, while on missions, Germans would broadcast in English an order on our frequency to "return to the base immediately," with instructions to fly in a certain direction. The voice was definitely American and the direction would be deeper into enemy territory. We were warned of this trick and never fell for it.

I had seen another trick on an earlier mission when they threw up green and red flak. It was meant to distract us from using flak evasion so they could have more time to track us with their radar. This trick didn't work either. It did not take much imagination to see through their tricks, but we gave them credit for trying.

Monday 29 January 1945

"The Mark VIII Optical Gunsight has four main parts: light source; reticle, a ring and bead stamped from metal or etched on the back of a mirror; lens; reflector plate – a transparent mirror on which the reticle image is projected. The reflector plate is a piece of glass about four inches tall and two inches wide; in the center when the sight is on, there will be a circle of light about an inch and a quarter in diameter, and a pin – point 'bullseye' or bead of light, no bigger than one – sixteenth of an inch. When the target almost fills the ring, release the ammunition."

Pilot's instruction on use of the gunsight.

During the Battle of the Bulge heavy fighting was evident everywhere, on the ground and in the air. Ground forces were up against wave after wave of everything the Germans could muster.

Every flyable airplane and every pilot on flying status shuttled back and forth on missions supporting the army. Instead of the usual three squadrons of 16 planes each, flights of four were sent, each in a different area with the order to "hit anything that moves" across the bomb line, or "targets of opportunity." On occasion when a flight was assigned a particular target, the standing order to hit anything that moved still prevailed.

Snow still covered the ground on a sunny day when I was flying element leader in Joe Wilson's flight. The flight went to its assigned target near Honnef and bombed and strafed two barges and two military transports. That done, we headed back to base looking for other available targets.

Indiscriminate bombing or strafing of towns was not the normal course of business. It was assumed, however, that all traffic on the roads carried some military personnel or objects of war, and these were fair game for targets of opportunity. Shooting civilians, of course, was forbidden, but when one is constantly bombarded with training to fight and hunt it can become an obsession.

En route back to the base at about 2,000 feet, there were two people working near a rock farmhouse, going about their business of farming. Remembering our orders, I broke away from the flight and dived toward them adjusting my P–47 to center the targets in my gunsight.

At first they did not seem afraid of the plane diving toward them, apparently thinking that any civilized human would not harm unarmed persons. They were waiting for me to recognize them as farmers, wobble my wings in a salute and pull up without firing, as might have happened before.

I continued coming down, hypnotized by the pipper in the gunsight, and they began running when they realized it was my intention to shoot them.

They were getting larger and larger in my gunsight, until it seemed that I would ram them instead of shoot them. I squeezed the trigger and let off a one second burst of the guns. In the circle of light I could see them round the corner of the rock farmhouse, unharmed.

At that instant I snapped out of my trance and realized what I had just done. Pulling up from the dive, I could feel my whole body flush and felt both hot and cold at the same time. I had never before, nor since, been as ashamed as I was at that moment.

In the years following this incident I have thought about it many times and thanked God for my poor marksmanship that day.

Thursday 1 February 1945

"By the end of January the Bulge was eliminated at a cost which proved fatal to the enemy. In the single day of 22 January, the Air Force destroyed or damaged

more than 4,192 pieces of heavy equipment, including locomotives, rail cars, tanks and motor and horse–drawn vehicles. The Germans lost 220,000 men, including 110,000 prisoners."

General George C. Marshall's
report to the Secretary of War

The battle for the Ardennes, the Bulge, was over, and the initiative had switched to the Allies. Despite bad weather, close coordination between air and ground troops was vital in the Allies' victorious push. Maj. Gen. Anthony McAullife, Commander of the 101st Airborne Division, defender of Bastogne, expressed his appreciation of air support, saying,

"If it had not been for your splendid cooperation we should never have been able to hold out. We were able to hold the vital road junction at Bastogne with your aid. I thought flak in Holland was bad, but the stuff your boys flew through was much worse."

Due to the bad weather, even worse now, we did not expect to fly. Dive bombing cannot be done if targets can't be seen, and a 10/10 cloud cover stretched from 2,000 feet to 7,000 feet, from our base to the target area. Nevertheless, all pilots scheduled for the first mission had to be prepared to fly as if the weather were CAVU (Ceiling And Visibility Unlimited).

The ready room was filled with pilots in flight suits, parachutes against the wall, visiting, playing cards or reading, waiting for the word that all missions were grounded for the day. Soon, the CO came into the room and called a briefing. It was not usually the way flying was called off, but we assumed he had something else to tell us before canceling all missions for the day.

He explained that the 508th Squadron was assigned a "pickle barrel" mission to bomb a manufacturing plant north of Frankfurt. We looked at each other wondering if headquarters knew what the weather was like here and over the target.

The CO continued, explaining what and where the target was, then the ops officer took over to explain how the mission would be accomplished. I had not flown a pickle barrel mission before and had heard about them as pertaining only to bombers, not fighters. But we were to give this a try and see if it would be successful. If so, we would be flying more of those bad weather missions.

The target and its location and distance were known. The amount of time to go there and back and the fuel consumption were also known. The briefing officer told what the bomb load would be and how thick the clouds were the squadron had to fly through. One thing was missing: we could not see the target. This would be a new ball game.

The ops officer explained that we were to go to the target area, guided by radar. We knew the elevation of the ground at the target, and our own altitude, and what our airspeed would be at that time. With some calculations, it was determined what the trajectory of the bombs should be if dropped from certain altitude and speed. Taking into consideration the estimated winds aloft at that point, the air resistance and so forth, we were supposed to know where the bombs would land. Some of the factors were known and others would necessarily be guesswork, but it was the best that could be done with what was available. It was important to know if a pickle barrel mission would be successful.

The briefing over, the squadron took off with two 500–lb GPs on the wings and a frag under the belly, and climbed through the clouds to our destination. Nearing the target, the squadron leader was in radio contact with the ground controller, getting more explicit instructions about airspeed, altitude and directions from the ground. The squadron's battle formation was pulled in to a tight formation for the bombs to be concentrated on the target when released.

Ground control guided us to a point where two radio beams intersected over the target, and at that point, told us to release our bombs simultaneously. When we got there, we were given the order, and Bombs Away! Into the clouds.

It was a hollow feeling when the bombs were dropped. Nothing happened to tell us whether the mission was successful or not. No explosion could be seen. No smoke came through the clouds from the ground 7,000 feet below, and, no elation of a successful mission accomplished. Was it successful? We couldn't tell. The mission was completed with nothing to do but go home.

Next day it was reported that the pickle barrel mission was a partial success. I never knew what partial success meant, but I guessed that it was we missed the target but scared the enemy. It was apparently successful enough to fly a few more pickle barrel missions when bad weather warranted it.

Saturday 3 February 1945
Ahr Valley rail lines at Dumpelfeld and Kreuzberg. Caught flak. Hole in plane.

Thursday 23 February 1945

From the pickle barrel mission until now, we had been getting fewer replacement pilots, and those eligible to return home were asked to volunteer to stay longer. There could be only one winner in the war, and I believe even the Germans knew which side it would be. But not knowing when, we continued fighting and flying more missions than before because the weather cooperated.

A new Allied offensive was in the making and had already begun. Our activity was heavy anytime the weather permitted, so the increase in flying did not give much clue as to a big, new offensive, but we did notice many more heavies going over than usual.

The English Channel was the first big hurdle towards Allied victory. The march through France, Belgium and a foothold in Germany was so swift that it seemed the Allies could go all the way to Berlin before slowing down. Crossing rivers running generally north and south presented problems, and the Germans dug their heels deep to keep us from advancing beyond them. Winter and the Battle of the Bulge slowed down the race through Europe but the fighting was still fierce and determined. That was the time the tacticians determined to gear up again for an aggressive push toward their goal of Berlin.

The Meuse River forming the Belgian–Holland border had been crossed, and the next river to cross was the Roer, some 90 miles east of our field, but the big one was the Rhine.

All night and all next day we heard the drone of airplanes going over, night fighters and bombers, and just about anything that could be flown. The planes were both American and British and we knew something big was going on, as activity on our field had also intensified.

Operation "Clarion" was a 6,000 fighter and bomber mission to paralyze German railroads in preparation for the crossing of the Roer on the way to the Rhine. During the day, the 404th Group joined other Thunderbolt, Mustang and Lightning groups with flights shuttling back and forth bombing and strafing anything that moved across the bomb line.

The assignment of the 404th was to destroy flak positions the medium bombers expected to encounter. Every flyable plane was in the air, so the odd number of fifty–one P–47s from the three squadrons and a fourth composite squadron was to cover 1,000 square miles north of Frankfurt and conduct an armed recon in that area.

Most missions ranged from one to two and a half hours long and the configuration of armament and external fuel tanks were varied to fit the mission. A short mission might require the maximum armament, which, in our squadron, was usually two 500–lb bombs, one 260–lb fragmentation bomb, eight rockets and eight .50 caliber machine guns in the wings.

Longer missions needed more fuel than the 305 internal gallons, so some or all of the bombs were replaced by external fuel tanks. For missions calling for a longer range, a 200–gallon belly tank replaced the frag bomb. On much longer missions, the wing bombs were replaced by two 150–gallon auxiliary tanks under the wings and a 500–lb bomb under the belly, so the ordnance possibilities of the Thunderbolt were great.

With external fuel tanks, the weight of the load could increase by almost 2,000 pounds. The baffles in the auxiliary tanks did not quite keep the gas from sloshing around as they were designed to, yawing the plane noticeably if not flown straight.

We had taken off in light cloud cover, with the weather over the target predicted to be mostly clear. It was to be a long mission and the two 150–gallon auxiliary wing tanks and a 500–lb bomb under the belly was over 1,000 pounds more than our normal load. The longer takeoff roll took more care and the sloshing gasoline in the external tanks made in–flight handling more difficult, and coordination of the controls was more demanding.

Reaching the bottom of the clouds, they had become solid. We went into a wide–spread formation to prevent running into each other as we entered the bottom of the cloud on our way to the top.

Close formation took full concentration since all planes must rely on the lead plane for navigation. In battle formation, each pilot had more independence and better control flying instruments in overcast. It was a great relief to go into battle formation once we were on our way to the target. I hoped all the others continued on a straight course but was never sure that someone wouldn't turn into me in the thick cloud.

Flying on instruments was not normally a chore but with the gasoline yawing the plane and not knowing just where a neighboring plane was made instrument flying a little unpredictable. That was when full attention was given to flying.

After a few minutes in the dense cloud, the wings began icing up and, although the artificial horizon showed an ascending attitude, the rate of climb indicator and altimeter showed no gain in altitude.

At that rate I would never reach the top of the cloud, and wondered if the others had already broken through and wondered where I was.

Military Power, called water injection, was the introduction of a special fuel mixture into the engine to give an extra 300 horses of power. When the toggle switch was pushed, the plane hesitated momentarily before the extra power was felt. I never hesitated using water injection when necessary but it was to be used sparingly and only in emergency situations, and this to me, was an emergency. I popped the switch forward and slowly began to climb. With the extra power, I broke through the top before any of the others. Soon, I saw a plane emerging from the top of the white cloud, then another and another until all were back in formation heading toward the target.

That beautiful, blinding sunshine reflecting off the white clouds was a welcome sight. I had often wondered: which is worse, the flak or the weather? Some statistics show that there were more planes lost in combat due to weather than by enemy fire.

A challenging job well done can be satisfying. When I broke through the top of the overcast, I was satisfied just to get through it safely, whether it was well done or not.

Group Commander Moon had pointed out before the mission that "Many of the towns east of the Rhine had never been hit before. I want every pilot to pick out good targets and make every bomb count. We want to show them what war is like."

After the critique, he said, "You see what I mean about all those little towns untouched by war? It's good to give them a little taste of it so they won't want another one so quickly next time."

During the interrogation, Colonel Moon reported, "Some trucks were parked alongside a number of slit trenches the Germans dig beside the roads. I gave the trenches a squirt from my guns." Major Marshall reported, "We got nine locomotives and all of them blew up."

The purpose of war is to defeat the enemy, not a game with scores to be kept like baseball, the team with the highest score the winner. But there are similarities. Scores are kept in war, too, in part for the encouragement of the players.

The news media's fascination for keeping score on military operations emphasized the numbers of enemy killed and taken prisoner, ships sunk or aircraft shot down, but targets on the ground were also important. Our ground targets were listed to fall in one of twelve categories: military transport, armored vehicles, locomotives, rail cars, gun emplacements, dumps (oil or ammunition) and several other categories including horsedrawn vehicles.

My personal score for Thursday, Friday and Saturday was one military transport, two marshalling yards, seven buildings, eight goods wagons and one rail cut plus various other strafing damage not recorded.

From briefing to interrogation, a pilot's intense concentration and constant physical exertion, fueled by adrenalin, would drain the body of all energy when the work was finished. He would be keyed up tight for eight hours straight, then completely relaxed afterwards. Two missions of about two and a half hours each with preparation for the next one sandwiched between made one very tired. Interrogation, supper, bed, in that order finished the day. Between supper and bed, I had hardly enough energy to write a letter I had been putting off too long.

A good night's rest, though, and I would be ready to go again the next day. I had better be, because I was scheduled for the first mission in the morning, and another later in the day.

With so many missions in such a short period, it was expected that some problems would arise. Don Swan encountered one when he was shot down and presumed lost; at least, for awhile. Don was flying Purple Heart Corner, the last plane in the squadron, when he was hit by flak five miles east of Duren, and had to bail out behind the lines. He was unhurt when his 'chute was caught in a tree. When he heard some Germans coming his way he hid his parachute and covered himself with branches. They came within five feet of him but soon moved on.

Don continued cautiously walking west. At one point he almost stumbled into a trench with more than 100 Jerries in it. Don reported, "Just as I saw them a guard shouted to me to halt, and slammed his rifle breech. I shouted 'Comrade' and waved my hand and kept on walking, expecting to get a bullet in the back at every step. But the sentry just said a few words in German in what seemed to be a pleasant tone of voice and nothing happened."

After seventeen hours of hide−and−seek, Don encountered an American sentry who challenged him. When Don asked to be taken to his commanding officer, the sentry did so, but didn't take his aimed gun off Don until he reached his commanding officer. Don said of the sentry, "He was a damn sight better sentry than that Kraut sentry."

Thursday 1 March 1945

My ideas, likes, dislikes, fears, etc, of combat flying had changed in stages several times as I acquired more and more missions. At first, I saw combat as a novelty and full of adventure until I had flown six or seven missions, then it became just another job, still with the adventure and challenge. It would always be that.

The next stage began when I was hit by flak. My plane had been bounced around before but never until then was there any damage. This changed my outlook toward combat to a real fear, not of being killed, (young men believe they will live forever) but to a healthy fear of being hit again by flak. Perhaps a better definition would be anticipation and respect for flak. All transient thoughts were erased from my mind when I was strapped in the cockpit and the mechanics of flying took over.

There was also a fear stronger than being afraid of flak, and that was the fear of fear itself. Before then, my prayers were selfish: "Don't let anything happen to me." I continued to come back safely except a few scares; but I still had my greatest fear – the fear of being afraid. It was getting me down until I started praying to God to keep me from being afraid and to help me do the best I could. From that time, I was confident that nothing could happen to me.

My outlook changed several more times as more missions were acquired, but I knew I would never be afraid of being in combat anymore.

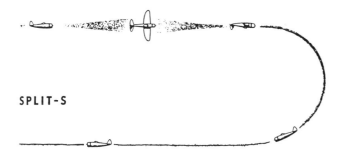

SPLIT-S

CHAPTER EIGHT

CROSSING THE RHINE AND BEYOND

Monday 5 March 1945.

The Rhine River was the next big obstacle on the road to Berlin. Bridges on the river that could not be defended, were blown up by the Germans. The Allies were racing to get to any bridge on the river they could take intact.

Although the weather had been bad, crossing the Rhine was urgent enough for us to get in the air for ground support before all the bridges were blown up. Our group provided air cover for the army as they crowded near the Ludendorff Bridge in anticipation of its capture. The group was to attack German supply and troop reinforcements on their way to the bridge.

Two days later, on 7 March, the Ludendorff Bridge at Remagen was captured intact enough for American troops to cross and eventually build a ponton bridge before the original bridge collapsed.

The significance of this bridge was not as apparent to us pilots as it was to those who make tactical decisions, but history records it as one of the major accomplishments of the war in Europe.

Thursday 15 March 1945

Joe was leading a flight and I was flying on his wing as we went to the Altenkirchen Forest. A P–51 pilot had directed us to a concentration of troops, trucks, tanks, a gun emplacement and other equipment. After we dropped the bombs and made a rocket run, we strafed several times, knocking out several tanks, trucks, flak guns and other targets. While Joe was at the bottom of a strafing pass, he was hit in the left wing by flak, and had a hard time recovering. He was so close to the ground that only a quick response kept him from spinning in.

He later said, "The first hit blew off my pitot tube and flipped the airplane past the vertical. It was all I could do with both hands to straighten out at 100 feet, and the Germans hit me three more times, once directly under the cockpit. Then I looked up and saw those two P-51s who had shown us the target screaming down with guns firing to silence both positions shooting at me. I thought I was going to have to belly in, but Kemal came in on my wing and led me to the field, signalling instrument readings to me. Once I tried to turn left and almost snapped into him out of control, but he peeled over me to the right side and stayed with me. I cut my switches and landed with a dead engine. Damage included loss of my pitot tube, a dent in the prop, a rocker box knocked out, hole in the oil cooler, all the guns knocked out on the left side, left aileron cut, trim knocked off, exhaust pipe cut, turbo pipe cut and numberless holes in the fuselage and wings caused by flak fragments."

The German gunners must have been amazed when they hit Joe with all they had and he kept on flying. Any other plane could not have sustained such damage and returned its pilot home safely. That was the biggest reason P-47 pilots had respect for the Jug.

It was about the same type of damage I got back in December when Bob Hurst brought me back on his wing.

Friday 16 March 1945

There was always one in every crowd; someone who was in the middle of everything; a friendly guy who always wore a smile and never took offense at the good-natured kidding he got, and never offended anyone by his teasing rebuttals. That was "Beaucoup," who got his nickname because of his short round stature. His handlebar moustache gave his round face with a wide smile a flattened appearance. He was the center of attention in any crowd he was in, simply because he was genuinely personable to everyone he met, and never seemed serious in any discussion. He was well-liked and thrived on flying missions, and would have gone on every mission if they had let him.

Beaucoup had "liberated" a German volkswagen and could be seen taxiing anyone who asked for a ride. When not on a mission, he could be found working on the volkswagen. It was his pride and joy. He was working on his car with Sully watching while Beaucoup waited for his scheduled mission later in the day. He became uncharacteristically serious while they were visiting and confided to Sully that he did not want to go on this mission today, saying, "I'd rather just stay here and work on my car." Sully didn't think much about Beaucoup's change of character at the time, but did recall his conversation later.

It had been just over a week since crossing the Rhine at Remagen, and there was heavy activity and a lot of flak on the east side of the river. Our pilots were coming back with a lot more flak damage than usual, and Beaucoup was on the last mission of the day. When the squadron returned, Beaucoup didn't make it back. He was seen bailing out and seemed to be alright, so we supposed he would be in a prison camp somewhere.

When the Allies overtook the place where he went down, they found his body in a shallow grave with twenty–two small caliber bullets in it. We surmised that he was shot by civilians from the ground as he was coming down. It is tough losing anyone, but harder losing a good friend.

Saturday 17 March 1945

I was due for the first mission being held up by weather. Sully and I were looking at combat film of some of our missions, when Robin suddenly burst into the room and said, "Let's go!"

Robin had been going steadily and seriously with Button, a Canadian nurse, and had discussed marriage for some time now. Getting two different nationals, in different forces, married in a country foreign to both of them takes more than a two dollar license and a blood test. The marriage had been called off indefinitely until the Belgian government, the U.S. Air Force and the Canadian military could agree on procedure. At this moment, their marriage was the furthest thought from our minds, what with a mission coming up.

After getting our attention, Robin explained that they had straightened out the red tape. We had to go to Brussels to get Button and be back in the Belgian mayor's offices in St. Trond for a civil ceremony by 3 o'clock, then on to the base chapel for a religious ceremony.

The first mission had been delayed for several hours due to the weather, and it was now past eleven, so Sully and I got excused from the mission. Brussels was over forty miles away, so the three of us made a mad dash in a jeep to Brussels. We picked up Button and returned to the waiting mayor and other officials of St. Trond in time for the civil ceremony.

Sitting around a large conference table with the mayor and several officials asking all of us questions, filling out forms and signing papers, it seemed more of a business transaction than a marriage ceremony. Only partly married, Button refused to give Robin the traditional marriage kiss.

Sully, Robin and I had been together for a long time and were the closest of friends, and since Robin had met Button, she too, became one of us. It was an unspoken understanding that Sully and I would participate in the wedding, but it was never discussed what part we would play until now. Robin and Button hurriedly agreed that Sully would be the best man and I would give the bride away because I was older.

From the mayor's office we jumped in the jeep and rushed back to the chapel on the field now filled with friends waiting for the wedding party to arrive.

Button was lovely in her officer's uniform topped with a jaunty beret, and Robin wore his dress uniform. Sully and I had been picked up at the ready room in our flying suits and, with the fast moving events, did not have time for a change of clothing.

Here's the scene: Robin and Button were dressed for the occasion. Sully and I in our flight suits and jackets, dressed for the first morning mission, steering a seemingly runaway jeep back to the field. We screeched to a dusty halt in front of the chapel, jumped out of the jeep and ran to the front door and stopped, not knowing what to do next. The chaplain saved the day by taking over. Sully and I rushed to our quarters to change clothes while the chaplain gave Robin and Button final instructions.

The second ceremony went smoothly and this time Robin was allowed to kiss the bride. We were still tired and excited and had not eaten since before dawn. They had just gone through what was to have been the most romantic event of their lives, and we were surprised at Button's first remark as we left the front door of the chapel.

Drained of all energy, but still excited, she said, "I'm hungry. Let's go eat."

Monday 19 March 1945.

"By 25 March hard fighting in the Remagen area had
extended the bridgehead to a depth of ten miles and

*a length of over thirty. . . .With solid contact between
their advancing corps, the First and Third Armies
were now executing a massive thrust to the northeast
into the heart of Germany. The complete rout of the
German   military   establishment   was   now
underway. . . . . ."*

*From General George C. Marshall's 1945
report to the Secretary of War.*

The bridge across the Rhine River at Remagen had been
crossed by the U.S. First Army over a week before, and the area was
bustling with activity eight miles east of the Rhine. The retreating
enemy was being overrun by the advancing U.S. First Army. The
two forces blended into a blurred bomb line making the maps on our
briefing board unreliable.

**Pilots from fighter – bomber groups were attached to ground forces
to help direct aerial bombardment and strafing. Ground
controllers would get information from the infantry and relay it to
the circling planes, making their strikes more accurate. (Leap Off)**

To help direct air support for the army for better accuracy,
pilots from fighter groups were temporarily assigned to serve with
the ground troops as ground controllers. "Sweepstakes," code name
for the 404th Group's ground controller, would be told by the
commander of the ground troops where he wanted the airplanes to
strike. Sweepstakes would then relay the message on the radio in
terms familiar to the hovering Group Commander exactly where to
drop his bombs and strafe. That almost always resulted in such
accuracy that the foot soldiers would report on the radio after an

attack, "Good show, we can walk in now!" or "Thanks a million, we'll buy the drinks next time we see you."

The group's second mission for the day was to go east of Remagen and give support to the army. When it arrived over the target area we were surprised to see so much vehicle and personnel activity on the enemy side of the line in daylight. Especially this late in the war when the enemy got the jitters and hid anytime an aircraft was heard. We called Sweepstakes asking what all the movement was. Sweepstakes answered, "Just a minute." Then came back on the radio advising us to "go ahead and hit it, it's the enemy. Good luck."

The Group Commander peeled off in a dive and began his run, followed by the rest of us. Almost as soon as we started diving, Sweepstakes came on the air urgently ordering us to pull up from our dive as the Germans had retreated from their recently-held positions and our troops had moved in. The U.S. troops replacing the Germans had not reported their position in time for Sweepstakes to give us the correct information.

Our leader, nearing the target in his dive, had already noticed that the insignia on top of the vehicles were clearly the white U.S. star, and had ordered the group not to drop its bombs.

He might have thought back to the time soon after The Invasion when the 404th Group was accidentally bombed by high-altitude American bombers mistaking our field for a German one. Several of our men were killed or wounded. This incident is told only to show how fast the Allies were moving once they had crossed the Rhine River.

Even without Sweepstakes' urgent order, we would not have hit our men, as we had already been given the order to pull up. The "what if" possibility remained with me, as it probably did with others on that mission.

Tuesday 20 March 1945

Our quarters at the chateau were comfortable. The pilots' sleeping rooms were crowded, but a large common room with a huge fireplace was furnished with tables and chairs. Most of the free time was spent reading, writing letters or just visiting in that room. Major Bob "Kelly" Garrigan had a three-room suite down the corridor from the room I shared with three other men.

It was evening and flying for the day was over for us. I had shucked off my clothes down to my undershorts to lie on my bunk and re-read some recently delivered letters. Sully came in to tell me that there was a party in progress at Kelly's suite and wanted to know if I would like to check it out. There was no need to be modest about our state of undress, so I jumped out of the bunk clad in only undershorts.

We went down the hall toward the sounds of the celebration where others, also attracted by the sounds, converged on Kelly's rooms. The party was going strong when we got there.

Kelly was at the door, also stripped down to his undershorts, as were some of the others, inviting and greeting everyone as each arrived. This was his big party. He had just been promoted to Lt. Colonel and wanted to share the happy occasion with his men.

As I got to the door he grabbed me by the arm and pulled me into the room where two steel G.I. water pitchers, surrounded by barrel tumblers, were on a table in the center of the room. One pitcher was filled with wine and the other with Scotch. He grabbed one of the tumblers and, shoving it into my hand, announced that his first order as a new Lt. Colonel was that his men would celebrate this occasion with him. Without giving me a choice of drinks, he filled my glass with Scotch and issued his first direct order as Lt. Colonel to me. "Chug – a – lug! That's an order!"

Never a heavy drinker, Scotch was not my favorite drink, and I was a sipper, not a guzzler. But an order was an order, so one did what one had to do. Without hesitation, I raised the glass in a toast to the new Lt. Colonel and chug – a – lugged about three – fourths of the Scotch before gagging and had to stop.

It took awhile for the drink to take effect, and I began getting drunk. Without another sip during the evening, I kept getting drunker and drunker as the evening wore on, until I could barely get back to my room to find my bed.

Later, when the effects of the chug – a – lug wore off, I hoped the war would end before Kelly got his next promotion.

Sunday 25 March 1945

In November and December, I flew from one to five missions per week, depending on the weather. Now that the weather was somewhat better, the group was flying more than ever to take advantage of it. In the past week, I had flown nine missions and expected to fly many more. Four – plane flights were often scheduled because they were more flexible and easier to brief. There were fewer large targets, and more small ones could be attacked by flights. That and the better flying weather accounted for more missions.

Our part of the war had not slowed down just because the Battle of the Bulge was over. It was apparent that the Allies were winning and it was just a matter of finishing the job. The Germans were still fighting and were not quite ready to give up. Some, however, in the face of the inevitable, did decide that it was time to quit.

A squadron from another group spotted a ragged column of tired German troops. When the squadron leader made a pass preparing for a strafing run, he saw nervous Germans waving white flags. As the P-47s roared overhead, other jittery Germans joined the first few. In a matter of minutes, there were about 400, all frantically waving white cloths.

The well-disciplined Germans formed columns of four on the road and were herded by relays of P-47s guarding them as they trudged off to Allied lines. The pilots radioed the nearest fighter control station to pick up the prisoners. That might have been the only airplane prisoner roundup of the war.

More bombs were being dropped, more ammunition and rockets were being used, and the group was running alarmingly short of bombs. Apparently the higher echelons had decided that the war was ending and had slowed down our supply of bombs, but we still had targets to hit.

It was about that time that we began filling captured German auxiliary fuel tanks with napalm, a mixture of jellied gasoline. They were rigged on the wing pylons instead of the 500-lb bombs we had virtually run out of. An incendiary bomb was used to ignite the napalm when dropped, causing amazingly destructive results against personnel or any kind of vehicle. Taxiing with napalms on the wings was done with care, as there was danger of one dropping off on a rough runway. It was better once off the ground.

Napalm tanks tumbled end over end when released, unlike regular bombs with fins that guided them on an almost predictable trajectory. Because napalm could not be aimed accurately, it was released from a flatter approach and at lower altitude than other bombs. Care was taken to pull up and away after its release because of its unpredictable path. On impact, it burst in a cloud of flame and spread like a bucket of water thrown on the ground, a beautiful but deadly sight.

Eventually, more bombs were sent to the group and less napalms were used.

Wednesday 4 April 1945

At A–92, the room four of us occupied with double bunks was crowded but comfortable. The warm air coming into our room from the large fireplace in the common room next to ours was pleasant in cold weather. If we got tired of shooting the bull in the big room all we had to do was walk a few paces into our own sanctuary. The chateau had inside showers and toilet facilities. We liked it.

The group had been there since late September and we knew we could not stay for the duration of the war, and would have to move on as the war progressed. We were anxious to finish the war and go home, so it was with mixed feelings when orders came to pack up and move to Kelz, a little village near Duren, west of Cologne and Bonn.

The engineers had scraped a runway in the mud and laid a pierced steel runway down for us to operate from by the time we got there, so the field was operational–sort of. The group had already begun moving to Y–54, Kelz, and my second mission of the day was to takeoff from A–92, St. Trond, complete the mission, and land at our new field at Kelz. It was our last mission from A–92.

I had already flown on the first mission of the day to bomb a marshalling yard north of Cologne, then on to support the Ninth Armored Division east of the Rhine River, returning to A–92.

The weather was good as we took off for my second mission to go to Frankfurt where there were some barges, a gun emplacement and observation post on the Main River. The weather had clouded up a bit when we reached the target area, keeping us below 5,000 feet. I was flying Red Four position, last plane in the flight. We were to hit the gun emplacement and observation post on the south bank of the river while the other flights worked over the barges.

The river at this point was situated in a valley between steeply inclining banks on both sides of the river. To approach the target from the north we had to dive at a somewhat steeper angle and pull up immediately upon releasing the bombs.

As we reached the target we didn't realize that the wind was as strong from the south as it was. When the first plane in our flight went on his run, his bombs fell far short of the target, in the river. The second pilot apparently noticed the short bomb drop and delayed his drop until getting closer, but his were also short. The third plane did the same and also fell short.

I finally realized that the wind was a lot stronger than we thought, and was determined that mine would not fall short, even if it hit beyond the target. I delayed my drop until almost on top of the target before pulling the release handle. The bombs fell on the target, but I had the advantage of being last in the flight and had gone to school on their efforts.

The mission over, we returned to our new base at Y‑54, Kelz.

LAZY 8

CHAPTER NINE

V – E DAY, MISSION ACCOMPLISHED

Thursday 5 April 1945

The comfortable chateau in Belgium had been replaced by cold, wet pyramidal tents in the mud. The group was to use an undulating pierced steel runway floating on mud instead of the concrete runways so used to. The recent German offensive had been put to rout and the Rhine River had been crossed in several places. It was time to move forward, closer to the war. The move was not entirely unexpected and the business of moving did not dampen the morale because it meant that the end of the war was closer.

Pyramidal tents were made as liveable as possible, and in two days tent No. 8 was one of the most comfortable in the neighborhood. A wooden floor, complete with rug, the tent held a wood – burning heater. The metal cots had springs but no mattresses, but were made acceptable with one wool blanket used as a mattress and the other as cover. The tent kept out the rain, and the stove helped neutralize the dampness and cold.

The mess tent was a half mile away via a mud path, but if we began to think we were having a rough time, we remembered our overnight stay in Aachen with the infantry, and were satisfied.

The candles had burned out and I had just finished writing a letter by flashlight about 10:30. I was trying to get comfortable on the cot when someone came into the tent and asked me if I was packed and ready to go. Packed for what, I asked. To go where? I was to go to the French Riviera on "flak leave" on the first plane in the morning. I jumped out of the sack and packed for my leave with Buzz Boy and Don from the 508th and pilots from other squadrons.

Flak leaves, or rest periods, were given when circumstances allowed. Sully and Elton had been to London a month or so back, and others had gone to Paris, Switzerland or other rest areas. Now it was my turn to go for a week of relaxation at Cannes, on the French Riviera, away from the cold mud to warm sun. A better time could not have been picked. I was not flak–happy yet, but I was ready to go.

Early next morning we boarded a bucket–seated C–47 wearing everything we could to keep warm and dry, and glad to be leaving such a cold, wet place. A few hours later we landed at Cannes, on the Mediterranean, where the boulevards were lined with palm trees. The weather was warm and sunny, opposite of the weather we had left.

Fifteen men donned in long woolen overcoats reaching below the knees and wearing heavy mud–caked flying boots deplaned. We seemed out of place in the balmy sun–drenched playground of the rich.

The army had taken over some of the finest hotels in Cannes and Nice as rest areas for its combat fatigued men. It was a world far removed from a war.

The next week was spent lying on the warm beaches of the Mediterranean Sea. Visiting the beautiful sights was much different from what we had been seeing the past year and the war was forgotten for awhile.

The leave was over all too soon and we boarded the C–47 back to reality. We were dropped off back at Kelz to find that the group had gone, leaving only a few men to clean up. They had moved to Fritzlar, nearer the front. We also learned the sad news that the day after we left, the squadron operations officer and three other high ranking officers in our squadron failed to return from an armed recon. They apparently did not see the side of a mountain in bad weather and flew into it. It was a tragic loss for the whole group.

Sully had stayed behind to greet us when we landed to take us to our new field. He had kept our personal belongings and had acquired a small German car in which we packed our gear to leave the next morning.

Saturday 13 April 1945

Buzz Boy took command of the driver's seat. The four of us with our gear, crowded into the small car and headed towards Fritzlar, 150 miles east.

About fifty miles from Duren we were driving along when the oil pan scraped a high spot on a bridge approach, tearing it almost off and leaking all the oil out of the pan. Repair stations were non-existent in Germany so we abandoned the vehicle in search of a more reliable one. Another was found, but was not operable without some new parts. We returned to the location of the one we had just abandoned to find that it had been taken away. It could not be repaired without a new oil pan, and chances of finding one was not even considered, so it was no great loss.

We were still a long way from our destination with no transportation, and it was getting dark. Recently occupied Germany at night was no place for American soldiers to be on the road alone. Every shadow was suspected of hiding a loyal German, and even trigger-happy American soldiers have been known to shoot first and ask questions later.

About dusk we encountered a Pfc in the infantry who invited us to his outfit for some food and a place to sleep for the night. The small infantry unit, operating somewhat independently, had taken over a small German tavern, complete with beer, so we Air Force men had a nice visit with the infantry that night. They gave us comfortable feather beds on which we slept two and three per bed, food, beer and a pleasant visit. It was not until after we had gone on our way that we discovered they had taken our warm flying boots during the night.

It was a good trade. Their hospitality, food, beer and a comfortable place to stay for our flying boots that we could replace. We would have gladly given them the boots if they had only asked.

Sunday 15 April 1945

We were on the road again, this time hitchhiking on convoys going to the front lines. The rides took us near a steel mill outside Solingen. Hitchhiking does not have as much class as driving one's own car, so we wanted another car to complete our journey. After rejecting several cars, including a coke-burner, we settled on a small panel truck to take us to Fritzlar. We approached the owner and simply commandeered the truck for our use.

Countries are either liberated or conquered by invading armies, and the rules of behavior are not always understood by non–participants. We felt at the time that we were justified in getting transportation in this manner to get us back to our outfit.

Now that we had our own transportation, the rest of the trip was made without further incident and we arrived at Fritzler that same evening.

The trip from Kelz to Fritzlar gave us an insight into the relationship between conqueror and conquered. The Allies moved through Germany so fast that the German people were dumbfounded and could hardly believe that control of their beloved country had passed from their German leaders to the Allies. They didn't know whether to expect suppression or compassion from their new occupants.

Before the Allies overran this part of the country, most of the Germans' movement of supplies was at night. Now people were seeing endless Allied convoys of supplies going day and night eastward toward Berlin. Bombing and strafing from the air and the shelling from the ground had stopped, and soldiers were now wearing different uniforms. German civilians' lifestyle had changed and was changing more, but they didn't know what the transition would eventually bring.

The orders from Supreme Commander General Dwight Eisenhower were not to fraternize with German civilians; to remain aloof, but a person's background will shape his response to such an order. In Oklahoma it is customary to greet anyone you want to, even a complete stranger, and these habits die hard.

On our way we walked through the streets of several German towns. Neither soldier nor civilian, when approaching each other on the street, knew exactly how to act toward each other. The adults were humble and the children looked at us out of curiosity. Some asked for chocolate candy. A few older men who evidently learned courtesy in a happier Germany, tipped their hats and nodded "Good Morning" when met, and we caught ourselves answering their greeting often in spite of the non–fraternization order. Added to the feeling of victory was another we were reluctant to admit, that of compassion.

The damage to the German towns was devastating and the destruction had leveled some of them, making them entirely uninhabited. Few towns had not been touched by bombs, and food was at a premium. The people lived where they could and ate what they could find. One night about dusk we saw some refugees stopped by the side of the road cooking what food they had over an open fire. The weather was cold and we knew they would be cold that night, and the next. The more I saw of this side of war, the more I thanked God that it did not happen in America.

We had recently moved from comfortable quarters at St. Trond to a mud city, and now going to somewhere unknown. We did not know what to expect when we got to Y–86, our new base at Fritzlar. It was a pleasant surprise when we drove into a large air base and were assigned rooms. The new quarters at Y–86 were reminiscent of St. Trond's.

My "private" room held only five men with space for each of us to have a cot, a desk and a small upright locker. Our sunny room overlooked the courtyard and we kept in close touch with the outside activities from our full length windows.

Prisoners of war and freed slave laborers, including some Jews, had been sent to Germany from their home countries to work in the fields and factories. Recently liberated by the Allies, they were used as much as possible for most of the jobs they could fill.

Thunderbolts awaiting repair at hangars at Fritzlar. Picture taken from a hangar roof.

Two French soldiers who had been held prisoners of war by Germany for five years were overjoyed to be selected to clean our barracks. Several Hungarian waitresses considered themselves fortunate to serve in our mess halls for only two meals per day and a place to stay. They showed their appreciation of freedom by their zeal to please their liberators, and went about their chores happily. Their moods affected our own attitudes and contributed to the high morale of the troops. Some of the DPs (Displaced Persons) were quite talented on the stage and performed a variety show in appreciation for their liberation.

With the flak leave out of the way and our side trip from Kelz to Fritzlar completed, it was time to settle down to fighting a war almost won.

Monday 23 April 1945

The Germans had retreated and all but disappeared from sight. Our targets now were generally inanimate, and missions to escort the brass going back and forth to negotiate surrender terms with the Germans and our allies, the Russians.

Most of the recent fighter sweeps and recon missions were concentrated near Torgau. My mission for the day was again Torgau, to escort C-47s with VIPs (Very Important Persons) aboard. We later learned that it was the site of the link-up of the Americans and Russians two days later. It was a clear, bright day and cruising with no flak to bother us and no ground targets to strafe was a pleasure flight.

It was obvious that the end of the war was near, but we did not have the slightest idea whether it would be sooner or later.

Tuesday 24 April 1945

SUBJECT: Order of the Day
TO: Commanding General, 70th Fighter Wing, all Groups this Command
The Battle of the Ruhr has ended with complete success, following hard upon the final destruction of the German forces west of the Rhine.....Over 317,000 Prisoners of War were captured including twenty-four Generals and one Admiral. The enemy's total losses in killed and wounded will never be accurately known... This victory of Allied Armies is a fitting prelude of Hitler's armies of the west, now tottering on the threshold of defeat.
Dwight D. Eisenhower

Tuesday 1 May 1945

Group Commander Colonel Moon assembled as many of his group as could attend to congratulate them and bid them a farewell, as he was leaving after a well–deserved return home. With Colonel Moon's departure, only five of the group's original pilots who had begun operations on 1 May 1944, one year ago, remained. Other original pilots were either lost or sent back to the States after completing their missions.

If any pilot was needed or wanted to stay, he would be kept on. Pilots who returned home did so because they had flown a prescribed number of missions entitling them to leave. Others elected to stay for awhile longer, but now that the war was virtually over, most of the high timers were sent back. All others were replacements.

When I joined the group, I don't recall any certain number of missions required, but later understood that any pilot with 100 missions was eligible to return to the States. Even that figure was flexible. None of the pilots that I knew of counted the number of missions to be completed for returning. On the contrary, we counted missions accomplished as we would birthdays, but not to go home.

During the Battle of the Bulge when every available plane was flown and every pilot was needed, "Twitchy," a diminutive captain with whom I had flown a lot, amassed his 100th mission and was eligible to go back home, but agreed to stay on as long as he was needed. Because he was a nervous type person, he was kidded a lot after his 100th about being even more nervous. (The name painted on the side of his P–47 was "Bundle of Nerves.") Let me hasten to say that his nervousness was not due to combat, it was simply that this was his nature. He was an excellent pilot and a pleasure to fly with.

It was obvious that the war was coming to an end as targets were insignificant compared to the earlier ones. It was time to total some statistics of the group's accomplishments. An accurate account of damage is impossible, but there are some interesting statistics compiled by someone in charge of these things.

In the year past, claims were 217 enemy aircraft, 6,152 locomotives and railcars destroyed or damaged. 1,246 tanks and armored cars, 4,697 motor vehicles were destroyed or damaged and other targets too numerous to mention. These claims were only the confirmed ones although we knew there were many not confirmed.

The group's losses were: 55 killed or missing in action. Five were shot down, evaded capture and returned to the base and nine taken prisoners of war. Not noted are the flak holes in the planes and countless close calls that, except for luck and the ruggedness of the P-47, could have been fatal.

Virtually every pilot was awarded an array of medals and commendations, and the enlisted men earned their share of awards for their hard work and dedication. Without the ground crews there would have been no missions. Of all the decorations and letters of commendations from the commanding generals, the most rewarding came from the thanks received from the men on the ground we supported. Their "Thanks a million, fly-boys!" let us know we did what we were supposed to do.

We looked back at the time spent in combat and felt that we contributed to winning the war.

Thursday 3 May 1945

Since the war was coming to a close, my last mission was uneventful. There were few targets left to hit and no more missions were scheduled after 4 May. The war was over for us before Germany's surrender was announced a few days later.

Monday 7 May 1945

We heard the good news of Germany's surrender one day before it was announced to the world. That night the air was filled with flare guns being fired. A celebration around a huge bonfire was held in the courtyard between the wings of the building. General Marshall sent a report to all forces announcing the defeat of the Third Reich.

> "On 5 May, the German commander surrendered all forces in northwest Germany, Holland and Denmark. Along the Danube, the Third Army continued the advance into Austria and entered Linz on 5 May. . . . . . At noon on 6 May, Army Group G, comprising all German forces in Austria, surrendered unconditionally to our Sixth Army Group, just eleven months after landing in Normandy. The powerful Wehrmacht had disintegrated under the combined Allied blows, and. . . .the emissaries of the German government surrendered to the Allies at Rheims on 7 May 1945 all land, sea and air forces of the Reich."
>
> General Marshall's 1945 report
> to the Secretary of War.

Tuesday 8 May 1945 V – E Day

> *"The long–awaited link–up between the Eastern and Western armies took place at Torgau, with the result that coordinated enemy action is no longer geographically possible. . . . Patrols of the U.S. 69th Division contacted the Russian 58th and 15th Divisions, and patrols of the 104th Division contacted the Russian 118th Division on the Elbe River.*
>
> Ninth Air Force Intelligence
> Summary, 30 April 1945

Tuesday 8 May 1945 was officially declared V – E Day. Special thanksgiving and memorial services were held to commemorate the occasion and honor the dead of both sides.

At that time it was not known what the group's next assignment would be. War with Japan was still going on, and rumors were that we would be sent to the South Pacific Theater of Operations. But for awhile, it was a triumphant time, everything else forgotten.

A bonfire at Y-86, Fritzlar, marked VE-Day, the end of war in Europe. The following day thanksgiving and memorial services were held to commemorate the occasion and honor the dead of both sides.

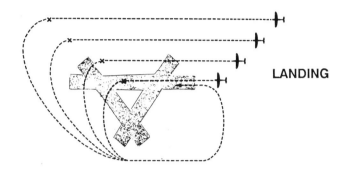

LANDING

CHAPTER TEN

V – J DAY, WAR'S END AND HOME

Thursday 17 May 1945

The South Pacific was still afire and it was rumored that the group would be sent there. At times, the military moved quickly, as it did at the beginning of the Battle of the Bulge, but now, we were to stand – in – line – and – wait. There was a slow – down of activity among pilots, ground crews and administrators at all levels in the group.

High – time and special situation men were sent back to the States. Robin was now married and had returned; men over the age of thirty – eight were released from active duty, and those left were kept busy preparing for a trip to the South Pacific.

Y – 86 was conveniently located on the airway to Berlin, and large enough to accommodate visiting VIP. Now that the hostilities in Europe had ceased, it had become a stopover, linking London, Paris and Berlin for meetings between the British, Americans and Russians.

High ranking brass in the Allied Forces were regular visitors at Y – 86. During the height of the war, Generals Eisenhower and Omar Bradley and Army Group and Army Commanders had come by to view our part of the war first hand. Generals Spaatz and Quesada of the Air Force knew our field well, and General Patton visited us.

Russian Field Marshal Ivan S. Konev, Commanding Officer of the First Ukranian Army, was scheduled to meet General Bradley here. As a show of friendship for our Russian allies, an aerial demonstration was planned. An aerial review was to be composed of the full strength of both the 404th Fighter Group and the 365th Fighter Group, stationed across the field and sharing our runways.

The mission was briefed as thoroughly as any combat mission had. Planes were to fly in a very tight formation, and each flight leader was to bring his flight in as close as possible. As in a chorus line of high–kicking dancers, one plane out of position would ruin the choreography of the mission.

Each group would have a full complement of 48 planes, a total of 96 Thunderbolts in a tight formation. One false move by an airplane trapped inside the formation could start a chain reaction of planes falling out of the sky. As mentioned earlier, the leader was the only navigator in close formation flying. All others kept their eyes glued to the next plane in line, and bad formation flying would cause a ripple of all planes following him. Nevertheless, close formation flying was fun because it was challenging. While it could be difficult, it gave great satisfaction when done well.

While taxiing out to rendezvous, before our final link up with the 365th, I was somewhat puzzled trying to imagine how the demonstration would work out. Taking off 96 P–47s from the same field, and rendezvous by flight, squadron and group took phenomenal planning. The two groups would then combine to form one immense formation, and their pass over the field was to be timed for the moment Field Marshal Konev would deplane. There was the possibility of so many things that could go wrong.

The timing turned out perfect and our first pass in review came across the field at 1,000 feet as Konev stood on the ramp.

After the pass in review and the two groups had separated, Colonel Garrigan led us through a wide 360 degree turn, coming back across the field at only fifty feet in a tighter formation for a spectacular buzz job.

Having flown in it, I find it impossible to explain the sensation and satisfaction I shared with the other pilots who were on this flight. It was as intense a flight as any in combat, and was the subject of conversation for a long time afterwards.

Because we knew what went into this flight, we were certain General Bradley and Field Marshal Konev would be impressed, and they were, congratulating Colonel Garrigan after the flight.

Colonel Garrigan is congratulated by Russian Field Marshal Konev after a spectacular 96 – plane aerial salute to the Field Marshal. (Leap Off)

Although we knew the flight was well – executed, some of the pilots agreed that simply completing it alive was an accomplishment.

Friday 1 June 1945

The end of the war in Europe had been celebrated. Flying was relaxed and training missions were flown to keep up our proficiency. There was a lot of free time and the men tried to keep busy.

Russ was the envy of some of us by flying a UC – 64 Norseman on mail missions. The plane was a nine – passenger (if it had seats), single – engine, high – wing, and Russ was assigned the pleasant duty of picking up mail at a central point and delivering it to our base. His dog, Turbo, was his co – pilot when Sully didn't go with Russ as co – pilot. Turbo was then demoted to second co – pilot. I often went along just for the ride.

The censorship of mail had relaxed since V – E Day, and I had discovered that Jimmie was stationed at a camp on the outskirts of Schleiz, a small German village near the Czechoslovakian border. Schleiz was so small that it was not on the maps we had, but it was near Bayreuth, about 55 miles northeast of Nuremburg.

Besides flying a few training missions to keep us in shape for our next scheduled assignment in the South Pacific, our activities consisted of loafing, reading and playing an occasional game of Hearts. Having found Jimmie and with hardly anything to do, I asked if I could leave for three days to go see my brother. Kelly said he could not officially give me any time off, but he would forget that I asked and not put me on any training missions until I returned.

That was all I needed so a musette bag was packed with a change of socks and a half-bottle of American bourbon I had been saving for this reunion. So Russ, Turbo and I took off and headed for Bayreuth, 130 miles southeast of Fritzlar. Russ dropped me off and agreed to pick me up three days later.

I found Jim's platoon in the 169th Infantry Division, but he was not there. He was playing in the band at a baseball game, so I hiked over there. The band was seated behind the home plate fence playing and nobody paid any attention to me as I walked behind them.

I spotted him in the clarinet section, and walked around in front of the band while they were playing, waving frantically at him. When he finally recognized me, he dropped his clarinet and clambered down to where I was, yelling to the band members that this was his kid brother whom he had not seen in over two years. Then we went to his pup tent to discuss everything that had happened since last seeing each other.

That night, Jim was guarding two U.S. soldiers accused of killing German prisoners of war, so I went along to make every minute of my short visit count. The prisoners were soldiers just like the millions of other guys who had been called to do an unpleasant job. Their crime was more of bad judgment. They were neither violent nor vindictive, and joined our conversation as friends.

The half-bottle of booze I brought to share with Jim was passed around among the four of us. When Jim's turn came to drink out of the bottle, he let one of us, me or one of the prisoners, hold his rifle while he took his swig. They knew he had a job to do and never attempted anything out of line.

The evening wore on and the bottle was killed by the time Jimmie was relieved of guard duty, and we retired to his pup tent. It had begun raining pretty hard by then, but a trench dug around the tent rerouted the rain, and kept the ground inside dry. This was another time I was glad to be in the Air Force and not on the ground.

Our reunion was over and it was time for Russ and Turbo to come to pick me up. Jimmie got a jeep and drove me to the airfield where we said goodbye, not knowing when we would see each other again.

Saturday 23 June 1945

Peace in Europe was about seven weeks old now. Practice missions and ground school in Japanese ship and aircraft identification had occupied some of our time. Playing cards and dominos and writing letters were popular pastimes. With other free time we took turns going to Eider – Zee, a rest resort, for a couple of days of boating, fishing and relaxation.

Now it was time to move on. The XIX TAC (Tactical Air Command) Headquarters wanted Y – 86 as their new headquarters, giving theirs to the Russians according to agreements reached earlier.

The author surveys German aircraft at a Kassel airfield. The Germans destroyed their planes before the Allies overtook this position.

The group moved to R – 50, near Stuttgart, back to a tent city. The weather was nice and our living conditions were much different than when we were in the tent city at Kelz. It was Spring and the weather was warmer and dryer, and loafing in the sun was pleasant. A different attitude spread throughout the camp.

During war, the dress code was casual but necessarily strict, dressed for combat. But in that tent city in the springtime with no responsibilities it was relaxed. Buckshot wore his silk top hat and loin cloth wherever he went in the camp. Men ambled to and from the oil‑drum showers in the nude with only a towel thrown over their shoulders. Squadron Commander Kelly Garrigan's tent, situated between the two rows of pyramidal tents, sported a sign advertising "Kelly's Bar Room," and welcomed any and all to come in and shoot the bull.

Dress code after VE-Day had relaxed to the extent that anything in a tent city near Stuttgart, Germany, was accepted. "Buckshot" chose this uncoordinated outfit, top hat and loin cloth.

Practice missions continued as we were still scheduled to go to the South Pacific, but ground school was stopped because of lack of facilities. We had more time on our hands with nothing to do but get on each other's nerves.

Hours were spent playing the card game of Hearts, and the longer we played the more serious the games became. Forgotten was the time it was played for fun, and winning was the sole purpose of the game. Scores were kept from day to day and the winner each day was sought out unmercifully to be toppled from his winning score. So serious did the games become that once when I gave Sully the Queen of Hearts, we refused to speak to each other for two weeks, but the games continued.

Kelly's Bar Room, Colonel Garrigan's tent near Stuttgart, after VE-Day, was always open for discussion. The sign at the top of the pole proclaimed: We specialize in baseball, hot numbers, hot pilots, hot pants, all kinds drinks. Sleepy Kelly prop.

Sully eventually realized what this was doing to our friendship and came to me one day. "Kayho, I don't know what is wrong with us, but we can't continue like this."

We didn't realize it, having been tentmates and roommates for two years, but our nerves finally snapped under the strain of inactivity and being cooped up so closely. Fortunately, the damage was only temporary and we continued our close friendship as always.

Sunday 8 July 1945

During combat we were all charged up and geared for any kind of flying we were asked to do. Every pilot in the Air Force had to ask to fly. It was considered a privilege to have been selected as a pilot, and we were eager to fly anytime we had the chance. If a pilot was asked what he thought about flying he would likely try to say in glowing terms of the joy of being alone in the sky to think thoughts not allowed on earth. If asked if he was afraid of flying he might reply with a look as if you were out of your mind. What a silly question. I had asked to fly, I was not forced to.

Fear of combat flying was another matter, however, a subject never discussed at length with anyone I knew. Aircraft maintenance in the Air Force was excellent and we flew with confidence in our planes, fearing only the weather and the enemy's armament, never the aircraft nor our own ability to fly it.

We had lived through our part of the war and now some of us thought it was time to be more conservative in our flying. We were going to the South Pacific and would get enough tough flying there, so now was a time for fun. There was a small plane, an L‑4, on the field and it flew like a kite. Flying it counted toward our four hours per month required flying time, and occasionally we flew it.

Some men believed that the end of the hostilities signaled permission to do some fun flying that we were not allowed to do during combat. Those were the pilots who buzzed prisoner of war camps at twenty feet. They flew under bridges, did slow rolls on the deck and other tricks limited only by the ability of the plane and the pilot's own ability and imagination.

Some tried other maneuvers beyond those limits. My own antics were limited to buzzing prisoner of war camps and other low‑altitude high‑speed flying, to see the faces of the people on the ground.

One of our pilots had distinguished himself during one single mission months earlier by knocking six German aircraft out of the sky, becoming an ace in one day. Destroying five enemy aircraft in the air qualified a pilot as an ace. This 20‑year old won himself the Silver Star medal for the accomplishment to be added to his other medals. Others in the group had the Silver Star, but destroying six enemy aircraft in the air in one flight made him special to us. We were proud of him, and besides, he was a hell of a nice guy.

Acting squadron leader was rotated among the qualified pilots, as the squadron commander could not possibly take up every mission. It was good training for men on their way up the ladder, so our hero‑ace led the mission today.

We took off and rendezvoused at cruising altitude, then flew a geometric pattern taking us to imaginary targets and headed back to the base. Returning, we were flying about 12,000 feet in battle formation when I had to slow down to keep from overrunning the squadron. All other planes had also slowed down to the pace set by the squadron leader.

Looking ahead, he could be seen doing slow rolls at very slow speeds. That would have been unusual under normal circumstances, but since V–E Day, the unusual became the usual, and his action was accepted as just another outlet for a pilot to express himself. Upon landing, he was asked what the hell he was doing. His answer was a smile that told us that he was simply having a little fun.

He confided to his close friend, Buzz Boy, what his plans were for the next day's mission. He had requested the leader's position again for the morning mission, and told Buzz Boy to pass the word to watch his takeoff. He was going to put on a show for the boys on the ground. The word was spread and a crowd gathered to watch the mission takeoff and see the show he had promised.

The planes were lined up in takeoff position when he gave his Jug full throttle and started his roll down the runway. He used all the runway to get as much speed as he could before lifting off the ground. Immediately upon lift off, the Jug's landing gear retracted into the wheel wells and it began a slow roll.

The spectators wondered what was happening and watched in shock as the plane made it through one–half of a slow roll and disappeared behind some trees beyond the end of the runway. We waited a few seconds for the other half of the slow roll expecting him to appear right side up and continue his flight. Three or four seconds later convinced us that he did not make it and had pancaked upside down. This was confirmed by the planes who followed him down the runway.

Each man lost in combat was a special tragedy, but wars were fought knowing people would be killed, and losses were expected. War was believed to be a reason for dying, but there was no understandable reason for our friend's death.

We had been ordered not to fraternize socially with the German people, but since V–E Day, attitudes between the Americans and German people had softened noticeably. Our friend's memorial service, held the next day in a German church in a small village on the edge of our field, was attended by almost as many German civilians as American servicemen.

Thursday 26 July 1945

We had been informed that going to the South Pacific was definite after a brief stay in the States. At that time, we just wanted to do something, anything besides sitting around doing nothing. We were glad when the long nerve-wracking wait at R-50 was over, and were ordered to a large assembly area near Rheims, France, for our trip back home.

Weary pilots loading up for a truck to take them to the Montclair Victory and a welcome boat ride home after VE-Day.

Thursday 9 August 1945

On 6 August the first atom bomb was dropped on Hiroshima, then another on Nagasaki on 9 August. Soon after, the Japanese surrendered and we knew then that we would not have to fight in this war again.

Thursday 30 August 1945

A couple of weeks at the camp, and a couple more at the port of embarkation at Antwerp, and we were ready to board ship. We didn't mind being treated as penned cattle because at last we were going home. Miraculously, the original nine close buddies who volunteered back at Minter Field, were still together, none lost to the war.

On 30 August 1945, we left the port at Antwerp aboard the "Montclair Victory," and headed home to the good old U.S. of A.

The "Montclair Victory Daily News" was a mimeographed one-sheet newspaper published aboard ship, noted more for its non-news than its news. However, the stylus-scratched headline on this sheet dated Sunday 2 September 1945 was the best news the world had known since 11 November 1918. It officially announced the end of World War Two, V-J Day, Victory Over Japan.

A bored but grateful lot of men relax on the deck of the U.S. – bound Montclair Victory.

END

MONTCLAIR VICTORY
DAILY NEWS

AT SEA   SUNDAY 2 SEPTEMBER 1945

JAPS SIGN -- V-J TODAY

ROUGH SEAS SLOW "MONTCLAIR"; "MILD" WEATHER, SAYS CAPTAIN

Rougher seas have slowed the "Montclair Victory" slightly to an average speed of 15.84 knots, according to Ship's Captain John L. Mobley. Total distance covered between noon yesterday and noon today was 396 nautical miles, he reported.

Today's swells the captain estimated as running seven to nine feet high.

"This is nice weather," he said, "compared to what we generally get."

This afternoon the ship was expected to pass south of a region of high spots on the ocean bottom known as "Faraday Hills".

MILES STANDISH DEBARKATION CENTER

According to an authoritative source, as soon as the "Montclair Victory" arrives at the port of debarkation—probably Boston—you will disembark and entrain at the docks within three hours. The train will take you to Fort Miles Standish, near Taunton, your debarkation reception center. From here you will be processed out to the reception centers which serve your home state or the state to which you are going for your rest.

LATE BASEBALL SCORES

American League:
  Yanks 3-3, Senators 2-1
  Athletics 6-2, Red Sox 3-4
  Indians 7, Tigers 2

National League:
  Cards 4, Cubs 1
  Giants 5, Dodgers 4
  Pirates 6, Reds 5
  Phillies 8-6, Braves 3-5

WORLD WAR II ENDED OFFICIALLY TODAY AT APPROXIMATELY 0900 HOURS JAPANESE TIME, ABOARD THE USS MISSOURI IN TOKYO BAY, EXACTLY SIX YEARS TO THE DAY FROM THE TIME GERMANY DECLARED WAR IN EUROPE.

Immediately after the signing of the documents in Tokyo Bay, President Truman went on the air from Washington to officially proclaim today, Sunday, September 2, as "V-J" Day.

Aboard the "Montclair Victory", Ship's Captain John L. Mobley, of Brooklyn, N. Y., heard the president's announcement shortly before three o'clock this morning. When the World War ended, this ship and its passengers were at 49 degrees, 38 minutes north latitude, 24 degrees 1 minute west longitude, 1143 nautical miles out of Antwerp and approximately 1978 miles from Boston lightship.

The signing of the peace terms took place on the forward starboard deck of the "Missouri" according to the traditions of the sea. A wooden box had been constructed to cover the peace papers in case of rain but the sun broke through the clouds majestically just as General MacArthur firmly and formally declared the proceedings closed. The Stars and Stripes flying over the "Missouri" at the time of the signing were those that had flown over Washington December 7, 1941.

Two Japanese representatives signed the surrender documents in the presence of more than 100 high-ranking American officials. Signing for the Japanese were Foreign Minister Shigemitsu and General Yoshijiro of the Japanese General Staff. General MacArthur was the first to sign for the Allied powers, followed by Lieut. Gen. Jonathan Wainwright, who had signed the surrender terms at Bataan in April, 1942, and other Allied representatives. Each signer signed two documents, one in English and one in Japanese.

GLOSSARY

Abort - To discontinue a mission and return to the field.
Ace - Pilot who has destroyed five enemy aircraft in the air.
Ack-ack - See Anti-aircraft.
Airdrome - Airport.
Airspeed Indicator - Instrument that displays the speed of an aircraft.
Airstrip - Airfield, usually with only one runway.
Alert - Standby pilots and airplanes ready to takeoff immediately.
Ammo - See Ammunition.
Ammunition Bay - Compartment in the wing of a P-47 containing ammunition.
Ammunition Bay Door - Door covering the ammunition bay on top of the wing on a P-47.
Anti-aircraft - Ammunition shot at aircraft in the air.
Anti-personnel Bomb - Bomb for offense of personnel.
Approach - Final glide path in the landing of an airplane.
Arm - Action taken to allow a bomb to detonate upon impact.
Armorer - Mechanic who supervises installation of ammunition on an aircraft.
Auxiliary Fuel Tank - Externally-mounted fuel tank that can be jettisoned.
B-4 BAG - Large heavy canvas traveling bag with several compartments.
Backpack Parachute -Parachute strapped on the pilot's back.
Bail Out - Jump out of an airplane with a parachute.
Bandit - Enemy aircraft.
Barrage Balloon - Unmanned balloon tethered by steel cables, used as protection over targets.
Battle Formation - Wide-spread formation of planes.
Belly Tank - Auxiliary fuel tank mounted under the belly.
Big Friend - Allied, or friendly, bomber plane, as opposed to a fighter airplane.
Bivouac - Temporary camp.
Blitz - sudden, overwhelming aerial attack.
Bogey - Unknown aircraft.
Bomb Line - Line dividing friendly and enemy territory.
Bomb Run - Act of diving to release bombs on the target.
Briefing - Meeting of pilots and leaders discussing plans for a mission.
Bridgehead - Protected position on the enemy's side of a bridge.

Buddy System - When two planes stay together to protect one another.

Buy The Farm - Term used when a pilot is killed in an aircraft.

Buzz (Job) - Flying low, usually for fun and not used as pertaining to strafing.

Buzz Bomb - V-1 rocket, unmanned German flying bomb.

CAVU - Acronym for Ceiling And Visibility Unlimited, and pertains to weather visibility.

Cletrac - Heavy equipment similar to a bulldozer.

Coke-burner - Automobile converted to use coke instead of gasoline for power.

Collaborator - Person friendly to the Germans during the Germans' occupation of their country.

Commandeer - Take forcibly for military use.

C-rations - Canned food to be used when prepared foods are not available.

Cowl Art - Pictures and lettering painted on the cowl of the airplane by the pilot or crew.

Crew Chief - Airplane mechanic in charge of the maintenance of the plane.

Critique - Review and criticism of all phases of a mission held after its return.

Displaced Person (DP) - Person left homeless as a result of war.

Drop Point - Point at which bombs are dropped.

Duffle Bag - Flexible heavy canvas bag to carry personal belongings.

Element - Two-plane unit of a four-plane flight.

Escape Kit - Kit of small useful items for use if a pilot is forced down.

European Theater Of Operations - Abbreviated ETO. European war area.

Fat, dumb and happy - Inattentive flying, oblivious of pilot's surroundings.

FFI - Independent Free French. The civilian French underground organization that fought the Germans during their occupation in France.

Fighter Group - A number of squadrons banded together, usually three squadrons in a group.

Fighter Squadron - One of a number of squadrons that comprise a group. See Squadron.

Flak - Anti-aircraft fire.

Flak Evasion - Weaving maneuver intended to evade anti-aircraft fire.

Flak-happy - Excessive stress caused by flak, making the pilot unable to perform to his potential.

Flak Leave - Temporary relief from combat to refresh and rest the pilot.

Flak Pocket - Area of heavy concentration of flak.

FPO - Fleet Post Office.

Flight - Four planes of a squadron flying as a unit, made up of two elements. See Element.

Flight Leader - Leader of a flight.

Formation - Any configuration of airplanes flying together.

Formation Takeoff - Two or more planes taking off together usually by element (two planes).

Fragmentation Bomb (Frag) - 260-lb. anti-personnel bomb.

GI - Government Issue. Means almost anything military. Often used to mean enlisted man.

GI Regulations - Military rules, regulations and policies.

Round Controller - Pilot temporarily attached to the army to help direct fighter-bombers to targets by radio contact from the ground to aircraft.

Ground Crew - Any member of the ground force who serve in any capacity to help maintain airplanes.

Ground Fire - Gunfire coming from the ground, including small arms fire and heavy flak.

Ground Support - Support supplied by fighter-bombers to ground troops.

Groundloop - An uncontrollable spinning around of an airplane on the ground.

Group - See Fighter Group.

Group Commander - Commanding Officer of a group.

Gun Emplacement - Gun position.

Heavy Flak - Can mean either a heavy concentration of flak, or large caliber aerial missile.

Half Track - Vehicle with pneumatic front wheels and rear chain track.

Hedgerow - Rows of hedge that divide tracts of land.

Horizontal Stabilizer - Horizontal portion of an airplane tail.

Hot Pilot - Facetious name given to a pilot who thinks he is a great pilot.

Hung Up - In fighter-bomber context, when an external bomb cannot be released.

ID - Identification.

Inline Engine - Engine in which the cylinders are arranged in a straight line.

Instruments, Flying On - Flying solely by reference to the instruments in the cockpit with no visual help from outside the plane.

Interrogation - Meeting held immediately after each mission to report and examine in detail the performance and results of the mission.

Jerry - Nickname for the Germans.

Jug - Nickname for the P-47.

K-rations - Food packaged in a box for use in the field when prepared food is not available.

L-4 - Small light aircraft used as an observation plane. Not equipped with firepower.

Leaflet Bomb - Bomb filled with leaflets to inform the enemy of information they might not otherwise have.

Light Flak - Small caliber gunfire from ground to air.

Link-up - Link-up in this context means when the Russians and Americans linked up at Torgau, cutting off German forces from further activity.

Lister Bag - Large canvas water bag with spouts.

Little Friend - Friendly fighter plane.

Lufbery circle - Circling maneuver of aircraft.

Luftwaffe - German air force.

Marshaling Yard - Gathering point for rail traffic.

Metro - French underground subway system.

Military Power - System whereby a mixture of water and alcohol is introduced into the engine to provide 300 extra horsepower in a P-47. See Water Injection.

Missing In Action (MIA) - An unconfirmed loss of a pilot during a mission.

Mission - A flight going across the bomb line to provide military action.

Musette Bag - Small canvas over-the-shoulder bag to carry small personal items.

Napalm - Bomb carrying a mixture of jellied gasoline that detonates upon impact, causing a burst of flame instead of an explosion like an explosive bomb.

Nose Art - See Cowl Art.

O'clock, One, Two, Etc. - System to describe the location of an object relative to one's own position, using the hands of a clock to describe the position, with the nose of the airplane as one o'clock. Three o'clock is 90 degrees to the right, etc.

On A Swivel - Keeping the head turning continually while in flight to observe and be aware of all action around him.

Operations Officer - Officer in charge of operations. Answers to the commanding officer.

Ops Officer - Abbreviation of operations officer. See Operations officer.

P-38 - Twin-engine, twin-boom fighter plane, named Lightning.

P-47 - Single-engine fighter-bomber airplane, named Thunderbolt. Nicknamed The Jug.

P-51 - Single-engine fighter plane, named mustang.

Parachute Rigger - One of the ground crew who packs parachutes.

Pass - Strafing pattern of attack.

Peel Off - Leaving a flight from echelon formation, one at a time, with the lead plane leaving first, followed by the number two plane, etc., usually to begin a dive bombing run or strafing run, or landing.

Pickle Barrel - Mission over total cloud cover, dropping bombs directed by ground control.

Pierced Steel Runway - Runway constructed by connecting units of steel panels over ground not suitable for the heavy usage of heavy aircraft.

Pitot Tube - Tube extending from the left wing of a P-47 (or other airplane) to measure air speed.

Primary Target - Target with first priority on a mission.

Ponton - (military spelling) Pontoon bridge.

Pyramidal Tent - Rectangular tent with straight walls and top the shape of a pyramid.

Radar - Radio detecting instrument. Acronym for Radio Detecting And Ranging.

Radial Engine - Engine in which the cylinders are arranged in a radial fashion as opposed to placing them in a line.

Ramp - Area of airfield used for parking or taxiing aircraft.

Rate Instruments - Cockpit instruments that rely on either the change of air pressure or the relative speed of the airplane through the ambient air.

Rate Of Climb Indicator - Instrument that measures the vertical speed of an airplane.

Ready Room - Room where pilots wait to go on missions, usually the same room where the briefings and interrogations and critiques are held.

Recon - See Reconnaissance.

Reconnaissance - Mission to search and obtain information from enemy territory and as a search and destroy mission.

Rendezvous - To meet another plane or group of planes at an agreed place.

Replacement Training Unit (RTU) - Base or school to train pilots for combat.

Replacement Pilot - Pilot sent into combat to replace other pilots who have left combat.

Rosalee - Code name for one of the ground controllers.

S-2 - Intelligence office.

Sack - Nickname for bed.

Scramble - Emergency takeoff.

Scrubbed - An eliminated mission.

Search And Destroy - Mission without a specific target. To go on a mission and search and destroy any target found.

Slipstream - The agitated air behind the airplane caused by the passage of the airplane through the air.

Slow Roll - Acrobatic maneuver turning the airplane in a slow rolling action in a straight heading.

Small Arms - Small caliber gun.

SNAFU - An acronym for Situation Normal All Fouled Up.

Snap Roll - Acrobatic maneuver that snaps the airplane in a quick rolling action from a straight and level attitude, making a complete roll and ending in a straight and level attitude.

Somewhere In Europe - Term used during the World War Two indicating the general location of an action without divulging the exact position.

Spare - Extra airplane that begins a mission with the same armament as all others to substitute for any plane that should abort. If none aborts, the spare returns to base.

Spin - Twisting maneuver of an airplane in a descending attitude.

Spin In - The action of an airplane that crashes as a result of a spin.

Spitfire - British single-engine fighter airplane.

Squadron - Unit of military aviation composed of three or four flights (in the 404th FG) of airplanes in flight. Also the full complement of personnel and equipment required to maintain the airplanes.

Squadron Commander - Officer in charge of a squadron.

Split-S - Maneuver beginning from straight and level flight, then turning to an inverted or semi-inverted attitude and entering a dive.

Strafing Run - Flight path while strafing.

Strip - See Airstrip.

Sweepstakes - Code name for ground controller.

Swivel, On A - See On A Swivel.

Target Of Opportunity - Any target not assigned, but worthy of attacking in enemy territory.

Taxi - To move an airplane on the ground under its own power.

Ten-in-one Rations - A box of varied food supplies to furnish ten men for one day's rations.

10/10 Cloud Cover - 100% cloud cover.

Tracer - Bullet leaving a visible trace of light when fired, letting the pilot see where the bullets are going.

Trigger-happy - Expression to describe the concept of a person eager to shoot with or without cause.

Trim - Cockpit controls that allow the pilot to adjust the flying attitude of the airplane.

Throttle Quadrant - Console housing the throttle and other control handles.

Thunderbolt - Official name of the P-47.

V Formation - Formation of airplanes that form a V shape.

VIP - Very Important Personnel

Water Injection - See Military Power.

Windscreen - British term for windshield.

Wingman - Second airplane in an element. See element.

V–E Day - Victory in Europe. May 8, 1945.

V–J Day - Victory in Japan. August 14, 1945. Formal surrender signed September 2, 1945.

Volkswagen - Small German car.

Yaw - To swing to the right or left while the airplane is moving straight forward.